Huldah

Lois Erickson

REVIEW AND HERALD® PUBLISHING ASSOCIATION
Hagerstown, MD 21740

The author assumes full responsibility for the accuracy of all facts and quotations
as cited in this book.

This book was
Edited by Richard W. Coffen
Designed by Helcio Deslandes
Cover art by John Edens
Typeset: 11/13 Novarese Medium

PRINTED IN U.S.A.

96 95 94 93 92   10 9 8 7 6 5 4 3 2

R&H Cataloging Service
Erickson, Lois N. (Lois Nordling), 1920-
    Huldah.

    I. Title.
            221.9

ISBN 0-8280-0671-7

Huldah

Chapter 1

Huldah, daughter of Barak, smiled as she made her morning plans. Her father had given her enough silver beads to buy a length of linen for a summer robe. Peeking out of her room, she glanced at the partially enclosed cooking area and other rooms that surrounded the small courtyard. Seeing neither her mother nor the maidservant, Kezia, nor the gatekeeper, Samuel, she slipped out quickly and pulled open the solid sycamore gate that led to the street.

She wore a green woolen robe that reached to the top of her tan leather sandals. A soft, cream-colored shawl, embroidered with yellow and orange yarn, covered her head and long brown hair. The silver beads rested comfortably in a small pouch she had tucked into a wide sash at her waist.

Already at this early hour the people of Jerusalem were leaving their homes and heading toward the noisy marketplace. Huldah pulled the large shawl more snugly around her shoulders. The street was a narrow canyon twisting between high stone walls, and the sun had not yet reached down to warm the passageway.

A short distance from her father's house, she could hear the merchants in the market shouting out their wares. She turned into the open section of mud-brick stalls where vendors sold food and peddlers spread their merchandise on the wide cobblestone street.

"I have a fine grade of almonds for you to buy," a shopkeeper called to her.

Huldah shook her head.

"Olive oil, pure olive oil," shouted the owner of the next shop.

She ignored him and continued in the direction of the linen merchants' street. Suddenly she stopped. Ahead of her at a grain seller's stall a young man in a brown robe was inspecting a basket of wheat. She frowned. She had seen this same man in the marketplace for the past three days. Not only loitering in the streets but watching her. Although she was accustomed to men's admiring glances, this man's presence annoyed her. Was it because he looked at her not with admiration but with curiosity?

To avoid him she turned into the street of basketmakers. Here baskets woven from palm fronds, reeds, or willow branches hung on the shops' walls and from ropes across the top of the narrow street.

Huldah pushed through the crowds of shoppers and into the street of clothing and fabric merchants, stopping at a linen shop. Mud-brick walls supported wooden beams for the closely-packed mud roofs. Three steps led up to the stone floor, and along the walls lengths of colorful linen hung from wooden rods.

"Welcome, welcome." The shopkeeper bowed to her. "You've come to buy at a time when the selection is at its best. Last week an Egyptian ship arrived in Joppa, and a caravan brought the linen to Jerusalem just two days ago."

Huldah fingered a white piece with an elaborate border in shades of yellow, orange, and red. A robe-length of blue linen drew her attention—until she caught sight of the young man in the shop across the way. *He's just pretending to examine that pair of sandals,* she thought. *He's really watching to see what I'm buying.*

The proprietor of the linen shop reached for the blue piece and waved it in front of her. "I can give you a good price for this one."

She shook her head. "Thank you. I'll not decide today."

Still waving the blue, he followed her into the street. "Look at this fine weaving. What will you offer?"

How can I concentrate on a piece of fabric when a man is following me around the marketplace? Huldah thought.

"I'll not decide today," she repeated.

Muttering a few angry words, he returned to his shop.

With determined steps, Huldah left the marketplace and hurried along a street toward the mount where the Temple stood. She glanced behind her but saw no sign of the man who had been watching her from the sandalmaker's shop.

The street ended at the top of a cliff. Below she could see the open area where homeless beggars spent the night. A path led across and up to a gate in the retaining wall of the Temple mount, where Solomon's Temple stood tall and majestic. Morning sunshine touched its cream-colored limestone blocks, turning them to gleaming gold.

Gazing at the temple she prayed, "Please, Lord, send us a good king who will remove the altars and statues of Baal from your house of worship."

Just looking at the strength and magnificence of the 300-year-old temple reassured her that someday the Lord would send a good king. She repeated her petition then reluctantly turned away.

As she walked along the winding street that led to her father's house, she wondered if the man in the brown robe was following her. Resolving to find out, she turned a corner and pressed herself against the wall. Shoppers on the way to market passed, and suddenly the man appeared around the corner.

Huldah stepped forward. "Pardon me, sir," she said in her most lofty manner. "Why are you following me?"

His body stiffened in surprise. "I cannot say."

She met the gaze of his dark brown eyes. "You've been watching me in the marketplace."

"Yes, I have."

"Why?"

He rubbed his neatly-trimmed black beard. "I needed to know more about you."

For a moment she struggled to regain her composure. "More about me? What do you already know?"

He stepped closer to her, but she backed away. "I know your name is Huldah. You're 17 years old and live with your father and mother not far from the Temple mount. Your father, Barak, is a scribe, and he has taught you to read and write. I know you come to the cliff every day to look at the Temple."

How did he know all this? What did it mean? She drew in a sharp breath. "Who are you?"

He smiled warmly. "I can't tell you. Not yet." Briefly his smile and his words distracted her, then she ducked past him and ran down the street toward her father's house.

At its high stone wall, she called, "Open the gate." As soon as old Samuel unbarred the heavy wooden gate, Huldah rushed in and slammed it behind her.

Her mother stood in the courtyard. She was a plump

woman. Now anxiety showed on her round face. "What's the matter? Why did you dash in like that?"

Huldah hesitated. Her mother was a chronic worrier, but if Abital couldn't find out the reason for her daughter's hurry, she would imagine the worst possible situation. "It's nothing really, Mother, only that a man in the marketplace was watching me."

"Who is this man?"

"I don't know. I asked him why he was following me, but he wouldn't say."

"You talked to him! It's not proper for a woman to talk to a man, let alone a stranger." Abital's voice rose. "Your father should never have taught you to read and write. That's why you're so bold and strong willed. Just because he has no son doesn't mean he should teach his only daughter."

Huldah stared dutifully at her sandals. "Yes, Mother, I know I shouldn't talk to a stranger, but he made me so angry."

Abital walked to the cooking counter where small loaves of unbaked bread rested on a floured board. "I've told you time and again to take Kezia with you when you go to market."

"When she goes with me, she always says she's tired and that I walk too fast."

"You're just making an excuse," grumbled her mother. "These are evil times in Jerusalem, and a young woman must be on guard." She poked at the loaves to test their readiness for baking. "But what can we expect when we have a corrupt king with a son who is just like his father? The only person in the palace who has any sense at all is Princess Jedidah."

"And her baby, Josiah," added Huldah softly. "Everyday I pray the Lord to send us a good king. Maybe Josiah will become that one."

Her mother sniffed impatiently. "He's only a baby. We'll have a long wait."

"Mother," Huldah confessed, "I didn't get the honey you asked me to buy."

"If you hadn't stopped to talk to that man, you'd have remembered. Now Kezia and I will have to get it when we go out."

Huldah looked around the courtyard for the maidservant. "Where is she?"

"Gone to the cistern for water. As soon as she comes back, we'll go to market. I must get ready. You finish the baking."

After her mother left the cooking area, Huldah turned her attention to the beehive-shaped oven in the courtyard. She used a shovel to pull embers into a stone pot before placing the risen loaves in the hot clay oven. Hearing a call from the street, she waited while Samuel let Kezia in.

"Heavy," complained the servant as she set the water jug on the counter. She was a short, stout woman the same age as Huldah's mother, in her service since their girlhood days. Through the many years their relationship had become more like sisters than mistress and maidservant.

Accustomed to Kezia's complaints, Huldah retreated to her room, her place for quiet times. The bed was a comfortable platform against the stone blocks of the wall. A table and a chair sat on the stone floor, and a heavy drape covered part of one wall. She pushed it aside and took a scroll from a hidden shelf. With the precious papyrus in her hands, her heart filled with gratitude to her father for giving it to her. At the risk of his life he had borrowed scrolls, one at a time, from a temple scribe and copied them for her.

How she loved to spend time in this pleasant room, reading the scrolls and pondering their messages. When a warm, sourdough fragrance drifted in from the courtyard, Huldah slid the scroll back into its hiding place. Using a wooden paddle she removed the crusty, brown loaves of bread from the oven.

Just before sunset her father returned from the scribes' quarters, his place of business. A strongly built man, Barak strode into his courtyard. He carried himself proudly, and his thick gray beard bristled with energy. Abital bustled out of the kitchen to stand close to her husband. "A man has been following Huldah around the marketplace."

"What did he look like?"

"Tell him," urged her mother, pushing Huldah forward.

"Well, he was young and . . ." Huldah checked herself. She had almost said that he was young and handsome. That's not what her father wanted to know. "He was young, and he wore a brown robe, . . . and he had a black beard."

Barak shrugged his broad shoulders. "So a man has been following you. What can I expect when I have such a pretty daughter?"

"But this is a strange man whom we don't know," Abital protested. "I've told Huldah again and again not to go out alone in the streets." She squeezed her eyes shut and tightened her lips.

Barak patted his wife's shoulder. "Don't worry. I can handle the situation. Now where's my evening meal?"

Huldah stared at her father. She had expected him to grumble about corrupt times in Jerusalem and even in all the southern kingdom of Judah.

Abital's mouth dropped open in astonishment. "How will you . . ." she began but after a glance at her husband's face, she hurried to the kitchen to set out the soup bowls for supper.

In the room where the family ate, clay lamps on the table cast a warm light. Kezia served cheese, bread, and honey, then brought steaming lentil and onion stew from an iron pot kept hot on the room's hearth. After taking a bowl to Samuel in the kitchen, she seated herself next to Abital.

By the time Huldah carried some lamps to her room, the night had turned dark. A low fire burned on the hearth, and smoke escaped through a high latticed window in the back wall. She was poring over a psalm of King David when a slight knock at the courtyard gate startled her. Strange. Usually a guest or messenger would shout a greeting from the street.

Huldah heard her father unbar the gate and let someone enter. She peered out her door, and in the flickering light of the courtyard torches, she saw the brown-robed man.

Chapter 2

The stranger was holding a bundle wrapped in a dark shawl.

When Barak walked toward her door, Huldah shrank back against the wall. "Come to my room," her father told her in a low voice. "I want you to hear what this man has to say."

Biting her lower lip, she followed the two men into her father's room. "Please explain to my daughter why you are here."

The visitor faced her. "My name is Shallum, son of Tikvah, who lives in southern Judah. I'm assistant to the keeper of the king's wardrobe."

Huldah drew back. What was a man who worked for evil King Manasseh doing in her father's house?

He produced a ring from his leather waistband. "I'm on a secret mission for Prince Amon's wife. Here's the princess' signet ring. To prove that I come in her service, she sent it for you to see."

Huldah stared at the gold ring he held between his

thumb and finger. Deeply engraved on the top were the markings that indicated the princess' name, Jedidah. "Why would she want me to know that you come in her service?"

Shallum returned the ring to a pocket in his leather waistband. "She asked me to find a young woman she could trust, and I have decided that you are the one."

"I don't understand."

"Let the man explain," urged her father.

Shallum took a deep breath. "The princess wants to obey the law of Moses, which says a firstborn son belongs to the Lord. The parents then redeem the child with five shekels of silver. Since Prince Amon worships the false gods Baal and Molech, he refuses to take his son to the priest for this sacred act."

Huldah's voice was a husky whisper. "You mean the baby Josiah?"

"Yes. I've met several times with your father, and we've discussed this situation. For Josiah's sake we must obey the law."

"What am I supposed to do?" Huldah asked anxiously.

"You and I will pose as the baby's parents. Tomorrow morning well before sunrise I'll bring Josiah, and we will take him to a priest at the Temple. The princess will also provide two turtledoves for her own offering of after-childbirth purification." He handed the bundle to Huldah. "She sent this disguise for you to wear."

Her father nodded his head. "Huldah will be ready before sunrise."

Shallum pulled his headcovering forward to conceal his face. "I must go now."

Barak stood up. "I'll unbar the gate."

Huldah remained alone in her father's room. She heard the sound of the men's sandals in the courtyard and the creak of the gate as it opened and closed. With her hands

14

against her forehead to still the turmoil of her thoughts, she sank onto a chair.

Her mother's voice at the door whispered, "I heard what that man said. How could your father allow him to take you into the streets at night?"

Huldah mustered enough courage to say, "We must follow the law the Lord gave to Moses."

"If you're caught, soldiers will kill the baby . . . and you." Her mother stifled a cry. "I worry so much. You're my only child, and I want to keep you safe."

Huldah stood up and put her arms around her mother. *For her sake I'll have to pretend I'm not afraid.* "That man Shallum will protect me."

"You don't even know him. What makes you think you can trust him?"

"Father trusts him, and he knows him better than I do."

With bowed head Abital returned to the courtyard. Back in her own room Huldah opened the bundle. A dark gray robe, rope sandals, a heavy shawl—the clothing of a maidservant. For a long time she lay on her bed, eyes open, staring at shadows flickering on the ceiling from the one torch still burning in the courtyard.

How brave the princess is to obey the law of Moses, she mused. *But how will Shallum find a priest before sunrise?* She pulled her blanket more firmly under her chin. *Can we do all this without Prince Amon or the king finding out that we're taking the baby to the Temple?* "Lord, protect that precious child," she prayed. At last her eyes closed and she slept.

Light and the strong smell from an olive oil lamp awakened her. She heard her mother's anxious voice. "Time to dress."

Huldah rubbed her hand over the coarse fabric of the robe. This was not the type of clothing she usually wore or would ever choose to wear. Quickly she slipped into the dull robe, draped the long shawl over her head, and fastened on the rope sandals. They would make little sound on the cobblestone streets.

A slight knock at the gate made her heart pound. By the light of the lamp in her father's hand, Huldah saw a gray-bearded man in a black robe and black head covering. She drew back toward her room. "Mother, I don't see any baby, and I'm not going with this old man."

Shallum walked quietly across the courtyard. "Don't be frightened," he said. "I have ashes on my beard for a disguise. It would be dangerous if anyone recognized me." He reached into a large pouch that he carried over his shoulder and lifted out the sleeping infant.

Huldah held the warm baby to her shoulder and gently stroked his back. For a moment she closed her eyes, and a shiver passed through her. Is *this really happening*? she wondered. Am I *really holding the future king of Judah in my arms*?

"We mustn't delay," Shallum warned. "We have to complete our mission before he wakes up and cries for his next feeding."

"Where are the turtledoves?"

He patted a smaller pouch.

Huldah frowned at the pouch. "I don't hear them."

"I dropped strong drink down their throats, and they're sleeping."

"Go now," ordered Barak.

Huldah snuggled the baby under her shawl and followed Shallum into the street. In the weak light from a half moon, Huldah could see his shadowy form. Although not as heavily-built as her father, he was taller and had a self-assurance that helped her feel secure. The baby breathed contentedly against her neck.

At each turn of the street, Shallum slowed to watch for

the king's soldiers who patrolled the city at night. When he came to the path that led down into the valley and then up to the Temple mount, he spoke quietly. "Now we have to proceed with extra caution. Soldiers rout out the homeless who try to sleep in the streets and herd them to this valley. All these down here look like beggars, but there might be some of the king's spies among them."

On both sides of the path she could see the dark shapes of the poor. Somewhere a child cried. In Huldah's arms Josiah raised his head. She patted his back, and he settled again with his head on her shoulder.

Where the rocky path wound steeply to a gate in the mount's retaining wall, Shallum took hold of Huldah's hand to lead her up. With the baby cradled in her left arm and Shallum's strong grip on her right hand, for a moment she could imagine that she and this man were wife and husband taking their child to the Temple.

Shallum stopped at the gate, and Huldah dared to ask the question that was bothering her. "Where will we find a priest?"

"As I explained to your father, I've arranged for a priest I can trust to meet us here."

They stood close together outside the bronze gate in the retaining wall. From here they were unable to see the Temple courtyard nor the Temple itself. A wispy cloud drifted across the moon. In the valley all was still.

Soft footsteps announced the arrival of someone inside, and then the gate opened enough for Shallum and Huldah to slip through. A priest stood in the shadows. A few feet behind him four Temple guards armed with swords and shields waited at attention.

Huldah tightened her hold on the baby. "Can we trust these guards?" she whispered.

"They're employed by the priests," Shallum assured her, "not by the king."

The priest nodded his head in recognition of Shallum, and then asked the ritual question, "What have you brought as an offering to the Lord?"

Shallum lifted the doves from his pouch and handed them to the priest. "We have brought these turtledoves to mark the purification of the child's mother."

He accepted the sleeping doves and slipped them into his robe's inner pockets. "What have you brought to redeem this child?"

"We have brought a bar of silver weighing five shekels. All these offerings we present according to the law that the Lord gave to Moses."

The priest accepted the silver. "And when the child asks why he was redeemed, you will tell him that the Lord slew all the first-born of Egypt but passed over all the first-born descendants of Israel. Then the Lord brought us out of Egypt. Therefore we sacrifice all first-born males of animals, but our sons we redeem."

"We will tell him," Shallum promised.

"Present him for the Lord's blessing."

Huldah removed the shawl from the baby, and Shallum took him into his arms. The priest touched his right hand to the baby's forehead. "This firstborn son is redeemed. May the Lord bless him." He continued to hold his hand on Josiah's head. "Yes, yes," he whispered, "I knew this child's great-grandfather, our good King Hezekiah." He looked up. "But go now. Quickly! I see the beginning of daylight in the eastern sky."

Shallum placed Josiah in Huldah's arms. She held him against her shoulder, and he nuzzled her neck, feeling for milk. Finding none, he whimpered.

Taking her by the hand, Shallum hurried Huldah down

the path and back toward the city. At the first street he paused. "I'll have to leave you here. We can't risk having him cry."

She gave the restless baby to him. Then he and Josiah disappeared into a dark passageway. She turned toward the street that led to her father's house. It too was dark and forbidding, yet faint color in the east warned her to hurry. How safe she had felt when Shallum took her to the Temple mount! Now alone in the silent city she anticipated dangers.

Suddenly she sensed movements. A furry animal brushed past her legs. She sighed in relief. It was only one of the many stray cats that roamed Jerusalem at night, rummaging for food.

As she neared her father's house, the stomp of heavy sandals on the cobblestones indicated a patrol of the king's soldiers. Too late to escape, she curled into the recess of a doorway and pretended to sleep.

The footsteps halted. A big hand reached down and yanked her, sprawling, into the street. "Why are you sleeping here?" a gruff voice demanded. "Take yourself to the beggars' valley where you belong."

By the light of their torches, she looked up into the gleaming eyes of their leader. She raised herself to her knees. "Please, my lord, my benefactor threw me out of his house, but he promised to take me back at daybreak. Could you, my lord, allow me to wait here for him?"

"Absolutely not!" shouted the soldier. "Get up or I'll push you all the way to the valley."

Slowly she stood up, and then behind the patrol another torch appeared. In its light she recognized her father. "Oh, my benefactor," she screamed, "you have come to allow this maidservant back into your house."

"Is this your servant?" the soldier asked.

Barak grabbed her roughly by the arms, "You good-for-nothing female, come with me so I can give you the beating you deserve." He pulled her down the street and into his courtyard, where she collapsed on a bench. He placed the torch in a holder on the wall and then touched her shoulder gently. "When I heard the commotion in the street, I feared for your safety."

"Thank you, Father. I'm grateful you came. The soldiers . . ."

"I heard them, but you're safe now. Did you accomplish what you set out to do?"

Huldah sat up. "Yes. It's done, and I pray that Shallum and the baby are safe also."

"I don't doubt it. He's a resourceful young man."

Abital stepped out of her room. "Are you all right? You look awful."

Huldah rubbed her side where she had fallen against the cobblestones. "Only a few bruised ribs." Thinking of the baby she had taken to the Temple, she added, "I'm fine and all is well."

* * *

Two days later Huldah again evaded her mother and Kezia so she could enjoy a shopping trip to buy the length of blue linen.

As she stood in the marketplace, gazing in at the fabric, the shopkeeper pulled it down from the wall and rushed into the street. "A fine piece of linen this one. The finest!" He held it in front of her. "It's the perfect color for a beautiful young woman like you. The blue sets off your lovely brown hair and eyes. What price will you offer?"

"I'm not sure," countered Huldah. "Perhaps the color is

too light." She hesitated, frowning at the fabric. "For what price would you sell it?"

After a lively exchange of words, the shopkeeper agreed to Huldah's final offer. She handed the silver beads to him, and he gave her the linen.

Huldah strolled down the street. No need to hurry now that a man in a brown robe was not following her. Her side still throbbed from the encounter with the soldiers, but it hurt less when she walked slowly.

Entering the crowded street of basketmakers, she considered buying a new basket to hold her sewing. One made of reeds caught her interest, and after bargaining for a price, she placed the blue linen in it.

Strolling again, she looked ahead . . . and into the eyes of a man striding toward her. Was this Shallum in the handsome maroon and white robe? When he stood in front of her, she could smell the sweet fragrance of lanolin and almond oil on his beard.

"At first I didn't recognize you," she confessed.

He chuckled. "I have another message for you from the princess."

Apprehensive, Huldah stared at him without speaking.

"She requests your presence in her chambers tomorrow morning." He paused. "When royalty requests your presence, it's not an invitation. It's a command."

Chapter 3

Huldah clutched her basket tighter and stared at Shallum. "Why? Why does Princess Jedidah want to see me?"

"That is not for me to say."

She searched his face for a clue. His smile told her nothing.

"Tomorrow at mid-morning I will arrive at your father's house to escort you to the palace." Without further explanation, he turned to go.

"Wait! Wait!" She dashed after him, bumping into a vendor and almost dropping the basket. "Have I done something wrong?"

He looked at her sympathetically. "I'm sorry, I can't tell you anything. I'm only allowed to deliver the message."

She watched his striped robe disappear as Shallum wove his way through the crowd.

The next morning Huldah woke up early. She turned restlessly on her bed until she heard Kezia striking a fire at the kitchen hearth. Leaving the bed, she knelt on a rug beside an acacia wood chest, in which her robes and shawls lay neatly folded. *What should I wear to visit the princess?* she wondered. *The yellow with red and orange embroidery? The blue and white stripes?* Finally she chose a sleeveless turquoise robe to wear over her long-sleeved yellow tunic. Orange and yellow embroidery decorated the neckline of the robe as well as the matching shawl. Trying to curb her uneasiness, she wandered around the courtyard. Near the kitchen a mint plant in a clay pot showed its bright green. She crushed a leaf between her fingers and inhaled its sweet fragrance.

"Come, eat some bread," urged her mother.

"I'm not hungry."

"Let her be," ordered Barak.

Abital sighed. "I've instructed Kezia to go with Huldah as chaperon."

"She doesn't need a chaperon to walk with Shallum to the palace," Barak said impatiently. "I wouldn't allow any man to escort my daughter unless I trusted him. He's taking her on a special mission, and Kezia would slow them down."

"I suppose you know what this special mission is?" inquired Abital.

"Shallum has advised me." Barak picked up a pouch that contained his papyrus, ink, and writing reeds to carry them to the scribes' quarters.

Abital sighed again. Huldah turned away to hide her smile. *Dear Father. Once again he has saved me from Mother's overprotection.*

At mid-morning a call came from the street, "Open for Shallum, son of Tikvah." Samuel scuffed across the courtyard to open the gate, and Kezia came to Huldah's door. "That man from the palace is here."

Huldah waited a moment to allow her heart to quiet its

beating before stepping out of her room. Formal and reserved, Shallum stood in the center of the courtyard. He spoke to her quietly, "This is not a secret mission, yet I ask that you follow several paces behind me through the streets, and we must not talk."

"I will do as you request."

In the narrow, twisting street, she hurried to keep up with his long stride. Occasionally he glanced back, but not even a hint of a smile crossed his face.

He led her into the valley and along a causeway paved with rectangular stones. Ahead the road wound up to the wall, high and thick, that surrounded the royal area. Many years before, King Solomon had built this fortified palace on a hill slightly lower than the adjacent Temple mount. At the entrance Shallum shouted, "Open."

"Who is there?" demanded one of the guards inside the wall.

"Shallum, son of Tikvah. By order of Princess Jedidah I have brought Huldah, daughter of Barak."

The gate opened. A palace guard, flanked by six others, scrutinized her and her escort. "You may enter," he said. In the expanse of courtyard that spread toward the huge palace, armed soldiers strolled around or sat in groups, but with eyes alert and weapons near their hands. They nodded in a friendly manner to Shallum and examined Huldah with undisguised interest.

Shallum walked beside her toward an inner wall so high that even the tallest man would be unable to look over. "Miriama will meet you inside the gate of the women's courtyard and take you to the Princess Jedidah."

"Miriama?"

"She's the princess' most trusted attendant." Two guards stood stiffly outside the gate to the women's courtyard. Shallum gave three knocks on the gate. It opened a few inches and a young woman peeked out.

He smiled warmly at her. "I'll wait here while you take Huldah to the princess."

Huldah glanced from Shallum to Miriama and wondered if they were just friends or something more. When the gate behind her closed, she gazed into a garden. Almond trees in full bloom wore clouds of delicate pink and white blossoms. Bright red tulips lined the walks, while beds of white narcissus perfumed the air.

"Come with me," said Miriama. Her rose-colored gown of the finest linen draped softly over her dainty figure. A scarf embroidered with pearls partially concealed shining black hair that fell to her waist. As she walked along the stone path through the garden, she turned her large, expressive eyes to the guest. "What do you think of Shallum?"

Caught by surprise, Huldah searched for an answer. "He's . . . he's very nice."

Miriama stopped under a tree and whispered, "He brought the baby to me that night so I could take him to his mother." Continuing to walk toward the palace, Miriama added, "The princess trusts Shallum. He's of noble birth, son of a chieftain."

No doubt you're of noble birth too, thought Huldah. Jealousy rose within her. *How can I expect Shallum to take notice of me when a beautiful woman of noble birth is interested in him?*

She looked ahead to the cream-colored limestone blocks of the palace. Now so close to her, it was even more massive than she had imagined. Two large Nubian women guarded the entryway. At her surprised gasp, Miriama explained, "Egyptians capture Nubians and export them to other countries. Prince Amon paid a high price for these two at the slave market." The Nubians opened heavy cypress doors.

Inside the women's quarters, Miriama led Huldah down a wide hall and up a stairway to the second level. From somewhere ahead the babble of women's voices invaded the hallway. The ladies of the court! The chatter stopped, and a hush fell over the room when Miriama and Huldah entered.

Many richly-dressed women lounged on soft couches or against cushions heaped on thick carpets. Their gowns were a display of colors, and their sashes vied for length of tassels. Jewelry of gold and precious stones hung around their necks, but most of all Huldah noticed the green copper and black lead cosmetics around the women's eyes. A heavy scent of perfume hovered in the still air—the spicy essence of cassia, the sweet fragrance of spikenard, the clinging aroma of rose.

Scarlet and gold tapestries covered the walls. Bowls of almonds and dates, and platters of rich cakes rested on sandalwood tables. In one corner a dark Nubian woman plucked a harp.

Miriama proceeded across the room to knock at a wide door. "May this one and a guest enter?"

A woman's voice replied, "Enter."

Huldah followed her guide into another large chamber. Miriama closed the door behind them and stood with her back against it. In this room the tapestries were more gold than scarlet, the rugs thicker, the pillow tassels longer.

Dressed in a blue silk gown that reached to the toes of her golden sandals, Princess Jedidah stood before her visitor. Her shawl of darker blue silk hung as long as the gown. Necklaces, bracelets, and the headband that held her dark hair in place were of shining gold. At her feet a sleek tan hound eyed the visitors.

At the sight of the luxurious room and the richly clad princess, Huldah's eyes opened wide in amazement.

Jedidah spoke softly. "Come closer, Huldah, daughter of Barak."

Huldah stepped forward.

"Closer."

Avoiding the side where the hound lay, she advanced again.

"In case someone is listening outside the door, I must speak softly," explained Jedidah. She glanced nervously around the room before continuing. "I want to learn more about the will of the Lord. I know the priests have copies of our history in the Temple, but I'm not allowed to see them. You have copies. Don't ask me how I know. I have ways of finding out such things." She clasped her hands tightly together, and her voice trembled, "I have chosen you to come to my private chambers every day to read to me. My mother told me as much as she knew, but I want to learn more about our ancestors and about the law that the one true God gave to Moses."

Huldah drew a sharp breath but said nothing.

"I can't read the scrolls myself. I don't know how," Jedidah continued. "We must take the utmost care. If the king found out, he could order his soldiers to execute us. To avoid suspicion, most of the day you will conduct a school for the ladies of the court here in these reception rooms. You will teach them to read from Sumerian writings. The king will allow you to use those."

"But I'm too young to teach court ladies," Huldah protested. "I'm only 17 years old."

The princess bowed her head. "I'm only 15, a year younger than my husband. The king arranged my marriage with Prince Amon in order to form an alliance with the chieftains of southern Judah. But I believe God has called me to raise my son so that someday he will serve as a good and faithful king. I need to know more of our history

27

and our law." She hesitated before adding sadly, "I can't read your scrolls to Josiah, but you will teach me how."

The girl's humbleness touched Huldah's heart. "I am honored to become the teacher for you and the ladies of the court."

"I will send Shallum to escort you each day. He and Miriama are the only ones who know of my plan. Everyone else will believe you come to the palace each day only to teach the women." Suddenly she stooped down and touched the hound. It sat up, and she put her arm around its neck. "Do you like my dog? You may pat him."

Huldah hesitated. Touch a dog! The only dogs she had seen were the wild ones that ran in packs outside the city walls.

"Pat him," urged Jedidah. "He won't hurt you. The pharaoh of Egypt sent him to my husband for a wedding present, but Amon hates dogs." She stroked its sleek, short coat. "I don't trust Egyptians any more than I trust Assyrians. Their armies have attacked Judah too many times. But I'm willing to accept this friendly animal."

Huldah reached down and gingerly touched the dog's back. It sat up and gazed at her out of deep amber eyes.

The princess stood and resumed her regal manner. "At each new moon you will receive your wages. Now you are dismissed."

Huldah bowed to the princess and backed to the door where Miriama waited.

At the gate Shallum spoke to Miriama. "I will bring Huldah every day." She smiled sweetly at him before she turned away. He led Huldah to the outside wall and across the causeway to the city streets. All the way her mind raced with questions. Could she safely conceal some writings to carry them to the palace? Was she, a commoner, capable of teaching noble ladies of the court? And not least of all—was Shallum in love with Miriama?

When they returned to her father's courtyard, Shallum warned, "You must take care to tell no one of this arrangement with the princess. As long as King Manasseh pays tribute to the Assyrians so they won't attack Jerusalem, he has ordered the people to worship foreign gods, mainly Baal, Molech, and Asherah." Gently he took her hand in his. "I don't want anything to happen to you."

Glancing into the intent gaze of his dark brown eyes, she managed a low, "I will take care."

Abital emerged from her room with Kezia right behind. "So you have brought my daughter safely home."

Shallum let go of Huldah's hand and stepped away from her. "Yes," he said politely, "and I wish to inform you that Princess Jedidah has chosen her to teach the ladies of the court how to read."

"Oh!" her mother exclaimed. "The princess has chosen her."

"Our own Huldah," said Kezia, "our very own Huldah. The daughter of this household."

Abital smiled up at the tall man standing in front of her. "Did you have something to do with this appointment?"

"After careful consideration, I recommended your daughter to the princess."

"How good of you."

"Each day I will come to escort her to the palace," Shallum explained. He glanced once more at Huldah before he went out the gate.

Abital smiled. "Such a nice young man."

"And so handsome too," added Kezia. "Huldah, I hope you are encouraging him."

* * *

Word spread fast among the gossipers in Jerusalem that Princess Jedidah had chosen Barak's daughter as teacher for the ladies of the court, and that she was using Sumerian writings.

From her scrolls Huldah copied portions on sheets of papyrus, small enough so she could hide them, one at a time, in a pouch under her dress.

Now when Shallum escorted her to the palace, she walked beside him. Always Miriama waited at the gate and exchanged pleasant conversation with Shallum before leading Huldah up the stairways to Jedidah's private chambers on an upper floor. Luxurious rugs, cushions, and couches furnished the rooms. Silk curtains covered the windows. Huldah could hear the voices of the ladies' children playing in a courtyard below.

But her attention centered on the baby Josiah. Propped against a silk cushion while she read and answered questions for his mother, he watched her with his bright eyes, and sometimes he smiled. Other times his head rested against the cushion, and he slept. With its slender chin on its front paws, the pharaoh hound lay nearby.

Huldah listened for footsteps and glanced frequently at the door, imagining she heard soldiers coming to snatch the three of them away to some dark dungeon.

When she left the princess' inner chambers each day to teach the ladies in the reception room, a Nubian brought a chair for her and Sumerian writings from the king's library—books that scholars had translated into Hebrew.

Jedidah sat on a couch, the ladies on plush rugs and cushions. At first her students' frequent giggling and the green and black cosmetics around their eyes distracted Huldah, but soon she thought only of the lessons.

As spring passed, almond blossoms in the garden

turned into green pods. Pink cyclamen and scarlet butter-cups showed their colors. Each time Shallum came to escort her, Huldah yearned for him to touch her hand as he had that first day. But he only led her to the palace and home again. Was it because of Miriama? Or some other reason of which she was not aware? In the street her mind focused on safety. Had the king found out that she was reading to the princess? She looked up at high windows and into passageways. Was an assassin waiting? Would a spear plunge into Shallum's back, and an arrow pierce her heart?

One day the ladies struggled through the words of a Sumerian proverb. "You go and carry off the enemy's lands. The enemy comes and carries off your land." Running footsteps in the hallway and a loud pounding on the door interrupted the lessons.

"Find out what this noise is," Jedidah ordered a slave.

The woman opened the door and a maidservant stumbled in. She fell to her knees and sobbed, "The Assyrians are attacking. They've crossed the northern border of Judah, and they're marching toward Jerusalem."

Chapter 4

The court ladies scrambled to their feet and ran screaming from the room. Jedidah shouted at the maidservant, "How close are they?"

Barely able to speak, the servant croaked, "Almost here." She turned and fled out the door.

"We must stay calm," charged the princess even though her voice trembled. "Miriama and Huldah, come with me to my private chambers." Leading the way into her bedchamber, Jedidah picked up her sleeping son and laid her cheek against his soft dark hair. "My baby, my baby," she crooned. "We won't let the Assyrians harm you."

At the sound of men's voices, Huldah stepped closer to the princess and Josiah. Someone flung open the door and a slender, brown-haired youth rushed in with Shallum following him. Each wore a sword attached to leather waistbands.

"Amon!" cried Jedidah. "We must hide Josiah."

"That's why I'm here. Shallum, prepare the place," he

ordered. "Miriama and . . ." He glanced at Huldah. "You, whoever you are, bring lamps."

Shallum pulled back a carpet and lifted cypress planks from the floor. Amon led the way down a stone staircase into a small room. All descended except Shallum, who waited above to replace the planks and the carpet.

Unable to stand up in the low room, Huldah and Miriama sank onto the thick rug. Prince Amon, fingering his thin short beard, and the princess, with the baby in her arms, sat opposite them. The hound crouched by Jedidah's feet.

"Where will Shallum hide?" Huldah whispered to Miriama.

"He won't. He'll stay with the king's advisors to observe the battle. When it's over, he'll come for us. This is the prearranged plan in case of attack."

"What if . . . what if he can't come?"

A sob escaped from Miriama's throat. "He . . . will. Surely he will come."

The two lamps gave sufficient light for Huldah to see water jugs and baskets of almonds and dates. Large cushions rested on the rug. The prince removed his sword from the scabbard and placed it beside him. "No one will take my son," he growled, "at least not alive."

While Jedidah gradually shifted Josiah to the side away from her husband, Huldah shivered at the thought of what might happen to this baby whom she treasured as if he were her own. No one spoke. The smell of lamp oil hovered in the stale air; only a crack between two stones let in a small amount of freshness.

With her hands over her eyes, Huldah listened for shouts from the courtyards or for the clatter of sword on sword, but the thick walls blocked any sound. *Why are the Assyrians attacking?* she craved to know. *Their empire extends from the Euphrates to Egypt, except for Jerusalem, but Manasseh pays a heavy tribute to their king.*

Jedidah timidly risked the questions. "Why are they attacking?"

Amon's anger flared. "My father refused to pay the latest tribute to King Ashurbanipal."

All fell quiet again. Huldah felt a tightness in her chest. Trying to breathe deeply, she thought of David's prayer as he fled King Saul. *O God, be merciful. . . . In the shadow of Thy wings I will take refuge, till the storms of destruction pass by.*

The wick in one of the lamps sputtered and went out. Amon uttered a short curse, and the baby woke up with a startled cry. While his mother nursed him, the sound of his sucking filled the small room. Huldah stirred restlessly on the rug, trying to picture what was happening outside the city walls, or maybe inside them. Light from the crack between two stone blocks grew dimmer and finally faded into darkness.

Footsteps overhead . . . and then the scrape of wood on wood as someone pulled away the planks. Miriama grabbed Huldah's arm. A lamp cast its glow, and Huldah swallowed in relief to see Shallum standing beside the opening. "The enemy has gone," he announced in a tired voice.

Amon was the first to crawl up the steps. "Gone! Our soldiers defeated them."

"No," replied Shallum. "They used treachery to defeat us and have carried off our king to captivity."

"My father. They've taken my father," the prince cried.

"Tell us how it happened," implored Jedidah.

"Their army surrounded the city, just out of arrow range."

Amon clenched his teeth and hissed, "Our soldiers should have gone out to fight them."

"The Assyrians had the advantage," said Shallum. "We know their bows are stronger and their arrows have a longer range. They sent messengers who promised that their army would not attack if King Manasseh brought the tribute. He and seven officials went out carrying the silver and gold."

"What then," yelled Amon. "Tell me."

"The Assyrians seized the king and the other men, bound them with shackles, and at this moment are marching north."

"We'll ride after them," shouted the prince. "I'll rescue my father."

Shallum shook his head, "Our commanders have advised against it. The enemy's too strong."

Amon reached to the neck of his robe and tore it to the hem. "This never would have happened if my father had allowed me to command his army, but I'm his heir and he thinks he has to protect me." He darted from the room, and Shallum hurried after him.

From the courtyard, women moaned a low wail, the wail of distress for captive men. It wavered through the air and entered the windows of Jedidah's chambers. It spread into the minds and hearts of those listening. Their groans united with it.

When daylight returned, Shallum walked with Huldah to her father's house. Soldiers—spears and bows at hand— crouched on the city wall. No other citizens made their way through the streets. At the gate to Barak's house, Shallum grasped Huldah's hand. "I will come to take you to the palace tomorrow."

His closeness gave her the strength she needed. She smiled at him and wondered about the intense expression in his eyes.

When she entered the courtyard, Abital embraced her

and tearfully sobbed, "You're safe."

Barak patted his daughter's shoulder. "The fortified palace is the safest place during an attack. Even so, those crafty Assyrians used betrayal to capture King Manasseh. I'm not sorry to see him go, except that Amon is worse than his father. What kind of life will we have with that young fool in charge?"

* * *

A caravan of traders journeying from the north brought word that the Assyrians had taken King Manasseh, not to their own capital but all the way to Babylon, a city they controlled. To appease the captors, Prince Amon ordered ten times as many sacrifices of bulls to Baal. The prosperity that the citizens of Jerusalem had enjoyed declined rapidly. With robberies and violence increasing in the city, Barak hired two men to sit outside his gate to guard the household during the night.

Now when Huldah and Shallum walked through the streets, she stayed close to him. In spite of new danger in the city, she cherished these times with her escort. While he dropped handfuls of wheat or barley into beggars' bowls, she waited. If she stopped to feed pieces of bread to hungry cats, he nodded his approval. Occasionally his arm brushed against hers, and his hand rested on her hand.

* * *

By the time Josiah reached his first birthday, he could stand alone, and holding onto the collar of the pharaoh hound, he took wavering steps. "My baby is growing up," the princess said to Huldah, "but I'll soon have another."

Huldah glanced at Jedidah's thickened figure. "Your time's almost here, isn't it?"

"Any day now Josiah will have a brother or sister." She gathered her young son into her arms and cuddled him on her lap. "It's common knowledge that Amon's father burned his firstborn son as a sacrifice to Molech. He threw him into the flames in the Hinnom Valley outside the city wall. If Amon has another son to keep as heir to the throne, he might take Josiah to the Hinnom Valley and sacrifice him to Molech. What can I do?" she cried. "What can I do?"

Huldah knelt by the weeping princess and encircled both mother and baby in her arms. "Can you send him to your family in southern Judah?"

Between sobs the words came. "My mother died when I was born, and now I've received word that my father is gone. I don't know what to do."

Later when Huldah left the princess' chambers, Miriama waited for her in the women's garden and gave a knowing smile. "Shallum is an important man in the palace with many servants working for him. King Manasseh's wardrobe holds more than 2,000 robes and 500 pairs of sandals."

Finding it hard to concentrate after the unnerving conversation with Jedidah, Huldah wondered why Miriama was reviewing this information. The young woman resumed talking. "What do you think of Shallum now that you've known him more than a year?"

What do I think of him? Huldah mused silently. *If only I could trust you, I would confide that I love him. He's not like men who have spoken to my father about me. The caravan leader who said he would burn his firstborn son to Molech. The scribe whom I was afraid might decide to worship Baal. I want a husband who worships God.* Aloud she replied, "He's a kind and thoughtful man."

"Yes, he is." Miriama stopped walking and lowered her

voice. "And he's clever in what he does." Quickly she resumed walking. "I've said more than I should. Please don't repeat it to anyone."

"I won't," said Huldah, trying to keep her irritation from showing. *Miriama is teasing me with these hints of something hidden in Shallum's life. Maybe she's jealous because he walks with me. But she has ways of talking to him in the palace or by the wall that separates the women's garden from the men's.*

Early the next morning a messenger arrived from the palace. "Prince Amon has a new son," he informed Huldah. "The Princess Jedidah requests that while she remains in seclusion, you do not come to teach the women of the court."

As soon as he left, Huldah closed herself in her room. *If only the new baby were a daughter, not another son to take Josiah's place in case Amon decides to sacrifice . . . oh, no, no, no!* She held her hands over her face to blot out the horrible thought of what could take place in the Hinnom.

Each day she hoped that Shallum would arrive with word of what was happening in the palace. Household activities occupied her time—baking bread, supervising women who came in to do the laundry, marketing with her mother and Kezia; but her thoughts turned often to the remembrance of Shallum's touch to her hand, his arm brushing against hers. Day after day, alternating between hope and dejection, she listened for the sound of his footsteps in the street.

"Why doesn't that nice young man come to see you?" her mother asked. "Just because you aren't going to the palace . . ."

"Huldah, have you been discouraging him?" her father demanded. "I'll never get you married off if you continue to discourage eligible men. I understand why you didn't want to marry the caravan leader, but I don't know why you

38

were disagreeable to that scribe a couple of years ago. I think word got around, and now you've done something to turn this man away."

"No, Father," Huldah protested. "No, I haven't."

Abital broke into the argument. "He's so well thought of in the city, and he has such a good position at the palace."

Barak put his hand over his eyes. "I would welcome a son-in-law who has some money. With King Manasseh in captivity, trade has fallen almost to nothing. That fool Prince Amon ordered a hundred horses, and the Cilicians refused to send them. The rulers of Cilicia don't want silver or gold. They want the linen and wheat we usually buy from Egypt, but we don't have any." He shook his head. "I haven't written a trade contract for two months. No contracts, no orders for goods, and only a few business letters."

"I'm sorry, Father," Huldah hesitated before she continued in a barely audible voice, "I think Shallum is more interested in a noble woman of the royal court than he is in me."

"You mean you've let another woman take him away from you?" Barak asked. "What kind of a daughter have I raised?" He plodded to his room and disappeared behind the door.

Big drops of rain splattered into the courtyard. "Come," said Abital, "we'll help Kezia prepare the supper." In a daze Huldah followed her mother to the kitchen.

Later in her room she drew near to the hearth and warmed her hands at the flame. Rain tapped a gentle rhythm on the courtyard stones. From the street came a call, "Open."

"Who are you?" demanded one of Barak's trusted guards outside the gate.

"Shallum, son of Tikvah."

Huldah heard her father cross the courtyard. "Let the man enter."

Chapter 5

Huldah listened to the tread of Shallum's sandals on the stones as he crossed the courtyard and accompanied Barak into his room. Their muffled voices reached her but were too indistinct for her to distinguish words.

She stared at the floor. *Probably he's talking to Father about the princess. Perhaps, even though her father died, she has decided to send Josiah to her tribe. Would she want me to take him to southern Judah?* Huldah covered her face with her hands. How could she and a little baby survive a journey across the Negev Desert—a place of great whirling winds, of vipers that crawled among the rocks, of robbers who attacked from behind the barren hills?

Standing close to the wall, she strained to hear what the men were saying, but their voices were too low.

Abital opened the door and stepped into the room. "That young man is here."

"Yes, I know."

"You'll be pleasant to him, won't you?"

Huldah gave a mirthless laugh. "He's not here on a social visit to me. He's discussing something with Father."

"But," her mother insisted, "if you have a chance to speak with . . ." A sharp knock at the door and Barak's hearty voice interrupted her. "Daughter, come to my room."

Huldah smoothed her hair and quickly draped a shawl over her head. At the door to his room, her father took her by the arm. "Shallum is waiting for you."

As she entered the room, he stepped toward her and reached for her hand. His touch sent a quiver through her, and her hand trembled in his. Looking up at him, she noticed an eager light shining in his eyes.

"The . . . the princess?" she stammered.

"Miriama reported to me that all is well with Jedidah and her two sons."

"I am grateful." She took a deep breath and asked, "What does she want me to do?"

"Nothing this time," he answered laughing.

Barak cleared his throat. "I have given this young man the privilege of telling you what he and I have discussed."

Shallum dropped her hand and straightened his shoulders. "Because my mission in Jerusalem has certain disadvantages, I have hesitated to declare my intention." Looking intently into her eyes, he stopped speaking.

Huldah frowned in puzzlement. His intention! Could he mean . . . ? No, he couldn't mean his intention for her.

"The time had come to speak to your father. You are the woman I want."

She was silent, unable to absorb the impact of his words . . . words she couldn't believe were true.

"Your father and I agree that you shall become my wife."

"Oh!" she gasped. "I thought you would want to marry

a woman of noble birth. I thought you and Miriama . . ." In confusion she glanced around the room.

Shallum shook his head. "No, not her. You are the woman I want. Let me tell you," he entreated gently. "When Josiah was born, Jedidah's father commissioned me to leave southern Judah, to watch over his grandson in Jerusalem. Of course, I'm not allowed to visit the princess in her chambers, so she appointed Miriama to carry messages." He drew Huldah to him, and then his arms were around her. "Only the princess knows that Miriama is my sister."

"Your sister! That's why she asked me what I thought of you." As she lifted her face to his, her shawl fell to the floor. At that moment she remembered that her father was still in the room. Turning her head, she saw his solid figure in the doorway, silhouetted against the glow of the torches. The rain had ceased, and he was gazing into the sky.

Shallum's eager lips on hers sent a shiver of excitement through her body. "Tomorrow I'll arrange with your father for the betrothal ceremony," he whispered. Slowly he released her from his embrace and then entered the courtyard to take leave of her father.

After he went out the gate and when Abital and Kezia finally ended their excited chatter about the betrothal feast, Huldah lay on her bed, pondering what had happened to her this evening. With a prayer of thanksgiving on her lips, she fell asleep.

The next evening Shallum arrived to discuss the betrothal arrangements with her father. They set the date for seven days later and agreed that Barak would provide a witness. While her father stood near the door to his room, Shallum lingered in the courtyard with his arm around Huldah's waist and his head close to hers. She listened to his whisper of love and raised her face for his kiss.

The day of the betrothal Abital and Kezia bustled around the kitchen, preparing barley and onion soup, roasted turtledoves, wheat bread, and raisin cakes. "If only he had declared himself last summer instead of in the spring, we could have served apricots and pomegranates," Kezia complained.

"Hush!" ordered Abital. "We're glad it happened any time of the year."

While they fussed about the food, Huldah retreated to her room. Already she knew she wanted to wear the blue linen. Now she removed it from the chest and lovingly smoothed its folds. She would always treasure this blue robe. Whenever she looked at the fabric, she thought of the first time she had considered buying it—that day she saw the man in the brown robe watching her from a shoemaker's shop. How irritated she had felt! And now he was the man she loved. Hugging the blue linen to her breast, she breathed in deep contentment.

While she dabbed fragrant lily of the valley perfume on her temples and wrists, she wondered if her father would insist on the usual one-year betrothal before the marriage ceremony. Such a long time to wait!

But still, a familiar worry returned; her father was betrothing her to a man of noble birth. Was she capable of living up to the duties of a nobleman's wife? Entertaining rich guests? Dressing in fine gowns and wearing expensive jewelry?

Dressed and ready long before Shallum and the witness were due to arrive, Huldah reached to the hidden shelf for a scroll. In the quietness of her room, she read, "O give thanks to the Lord for He is good. . . . Let the redeemed of the Lord say so." Her thoughts raced back to the night she carried Josiah to the Temple. Today in her joy and excitement about the betrothal she had forgotten to pray for the boy's safety. The reality of danger for the small prince returned to assail her, and she offered a fervent petition to God. "Lord, watch over him. Protect him."

Out in the courtyard, Barak paced back and forth in the sunshine as he waited for his guests. The scribe appeared first. He was of Barak's age but fat and slow moving. Soon afterward the call came, "Open for Shallum, son of Tikvah." Huldah's heart leaped, and hastily she replaced the scroll on its shelf. Old Samuel opened the gate.

She heard her father's greeting of welcome and Shallum's reply. Then their voices grew indistinct as Barak led the men into the dining area. Huldah stepped into the kitchen. "Mother, do you want me to serve the soup?"

Flushed from working over the fire, Abital wiped her face with a cloth. "Your father decided that you will sit at the table."

"I've never eaten with his guests before." Huldah's words protested, but her heart beat in happy anticipation.

"Your father has spoken. He says for this special occasion you will eat with them, but first he and the young man must come to some agreements."

Huldah withdrew to a bench at the far side of the courtyard. A shaft of late afternoon sunlight slanted across the top of the wall and touched her cheek. A slight breeze brought the warm smell of roasting turtledoves. She heard her mother in the kitchen stirring the barley soup, and Kezia taking bowls from a shelf.

Conversation from the dining room was low and guarded. At last her father emerged. She stood up and walked hesitantly toward him. "We have completed the betrothal contract," he assured her. "Shallum has offered a sufficient dowry for you. Also he will purchase a house and arrange for necessary servants."

"Thank you, Father."

"For my part I will provide your apparel and a marriage feast fit for a nobleman and his bride." He lowered his voice. "I have also agreed to an early wedding date—six months from now instead of the usual one year. Shallum says he has delayed long enough, and I think it's best to have you married before you're too old."

Six months instead of a year! She let out an elated cry. "This pleases you," declared Barak with amusement.

"Yes."

"Then let us celebrate." He shouted toward the kitchen, "Kezia . . . serve the dinner." Taking hold of his daughter's arm, he escorted her to the dining room. "Now go in and pay your respect to your future husband and the witness."

She took a deep breath and stepped into the room. Shallum reached for her hand and led her to the chair next to his. With him so close, she forgot for a moment the words she had practiced. Regaining her composure she managed to say, "Father, I'm grateful to you for arranging this betrothal."

Carrying a large pot of steaming soup, Kezia shuffled into the room. Abital followed with a platter of roasted doves. Then they brought loaves of wheat bread, raisin cakes, and jugs of wine. Bustling around the table, the two women served the men and Huldah. During the long, unhurried meal, she remained silent. Whenever Shallum looked her way and his lips curved into a smile, her heart sang.

At last Barak stood up. He faced Shallum and delivered the traditional words, "You shall be my son-in-law."

The younger man rose and, taking Huldah's hand, assisted her to her feet. From beneath his leather waistband, he drew a golden necklace and placed it around her neck. "See by this token you are set apart for me, according to the law of Moses."

With quavering voice she replied, "I accept your token." She heard her mother's joyful cry, and then the men's exuberant shouts filled the room.

The following morning Abital hurried into Huldah's room. "We must go to the wool merchant's shop for your wedding fabric."

"Yes," agreed the bride-to-be, "I want to start the embroidery right away."

At that moment Shallum's call came from the street. Huldah glanced down at the plain robe she was wearing. "I didn't expect him today. He said nothing about taking me to the princess this morning." When he entered the courtyard and she saw the pained expression on his face, she hurried to him. "What is it?"

"Josiah is safe," he answered as he took both her hands in his. "But when Prince Amon found out that I had planned our marriage, he decreed that no one from the palace shall marry until his father returns from captivity."

She clung to him and choked out, "That could mean years . . . or never."

He held her close, and she could feel his labored breathing. "We can't give up hope," he said. Slowly he released her. "Meanwhile, the princess has requested your presence. Tomorrow I'll return to accompany you to the palace so you can teach the ladies of the court." He turned away and motioned for Samuel to open the gate.

When he was gone, Huldah raised her head and pleaded, "Help me, O Lord. Give me comfort and strength."

The next morning Shallum arrived with a water pouch slung over his shoulder. "Some days I go outside the city

47

wall and offer water to travelers. If you would accompany me, we could have more time together."

She nodded happily. "I'll go with you."

She followed him out a city gate and down into the Kidron Valley on the east side of the Temple mount. They climbed a short way up another mount and sat under one of the olive trees. "We'll wait here," he said.

"It's so peaceful," Huldah remarked, "and a good place to look toward the Temple."

"Whenever I'm here," replied Shallum, "I pray that God will remember the people of Judah, that we will not always suffer. I pray also that before too long you and I can marry." He reached for the water pouch. "Some travelers are approaching."

She watched him walk down the hill and raise his hand in the salutation of peace. Here on the quiet hillside away from the city's turmoil, she could try to forget some of the disappointments and worries that plagued her. At her feet tiny white daisies blossomed, and a snail made its slow way through the grass.

Huldah watched while five men drank from Shallum's water pouch. Appearing satisfied with his task, he returned to escort her to the palace. When she entered Jedidah's chambers, Josiah ran to meet her. She swooped him into her arms as he laughed and tried to say her name.

The little boy's mother smiled. "Your name is one of his first words." She held a baby. "Come and see my second son." With Josiah still in her arms, Huldah stood beside the princess to admire the dark-haired infant.

Daily Huldah accompanied Shallum outside the city wall and sat under a tree while he offered water to thirsty travelers. Spring gave way to the heat of summer, summer to autumn. One morning she hiked with him to the top of the mount where they gazed over the hills of Judah. He put his arms around her and held her while she sobbed out her frustration over their lost wedding plans.

During the cool winter months, Shallum took Huldah directly to the palace, but when spring showed its first warm day, he invited her again to the Kidron Valley. While she waited under an olive tree, she noticed a flurry of migrating turtledoves flying north, and she thought of her betrothal dinner. Already a year had passed, and still she remained unmarried.

Before long Shallum returned from serving water to three men. When he sat down next to her, she wondered at the sad expression on his face. After some moments of silence he said, "These men have traveled all the way from Babylon. They bring news that the king of Assyria has agreed to release King Manasseh."

"Then at last we can marry!" she exclaimed in delight, but when she looked at him, he was frowning. Suddenly he held his hands to his head and a deep groan escaped from his throat.

Chapter 6

Huldah placed her hand on his arm and waited. Without looking at her, Shallum spoke in a hushed voice, "Prince Amon has promised that if ever his father returns from captivity, he will honor him with a great festival." He paused, once again groaning. "Amon says that during the celebration he will burn his firstborn son—the most valuable gift possible—in the fires of Molech in gratitude for his father's safe return."

Huldah cried out, "Not my baby, not Josiah!"

"You have to remember that Josiah is not yours," he admonished her gently. "He belongs to Amon. "

She stood up and scanned the valley. "Where are the travelers? You must stop them from telling the prince about his father's release."

"It's too late. They're already on their way to the royal court. They expect to claim a reward for bringing the news."

Kneeling next to Shallum, she grasped his arm. "Amon

mustn't sacrifice Josiah. What can we do to save him from the fires of Molech?"

Slowly he answered, "I have spent many sleepless nights considering what to do. There's a priest, a Benjaminite, in the town of Anathoth. He comes once a year to take his turn offering sacrifices in the Temple, and he offers only to God not to idols. We have become friends."

"Can you take Josiah to him?"

"I'll try, and if it is too risky to stay there, I'll journey east to the other side of the Jordan River."

"Is it safe to go there?"

"Any place is safer for Josiah than here in Jerusalem!"

Huldah bent her head to his shoulder, "It's so dangerous. What if . . . ?"

"Let's not think of what might go wrong." With his arm around her, he stood up. "Now I must take you to the princess."

"Yes, of course," she answered, but after hearing of Amon's plan, how could she concentrate on teaching? They walked in silence to the palace. When Huldah entered Jedidah's chambers, the princess was holding Josiah and singing to him. She stopped in the middle of her happy song. "What's the matter?"

She hasn't heard, Huldah realized. *If Shallum knows about Amon's plan, surely others do also. But no court lady or servant has been brave enough to inform Jedidah that her husband will sacrifice their son. Someone must tell her.* She took a deep breath. "I have just learned distressing news."

"Your father—or mother?"

Josiah wandered across the room to Huldah, and she picked him up. "My parents are in good health. The news concerns . . ."

A shout outside the door broke into her speech. The door crashed open, and Prince Amon marched in. "The

51

Assyrians have released my father, and he's on his way to Jerusalem. He grabbed Josiah from Huldah, and the boy started to cry. "My father will know that I welcome him home when I sacrifice my firstborn son to Molech." He swung the screaming child violently around and dropped him onto a couch. "Keep him safe and in good health until my father comes," he admonished Jedidah. "I want a body without blemish to sacrifice. I must offer my very best." He left as abruptly as he had entered. Still yelling in fright, Josiah sat on the couch and stared at the door through which his father had disappeared.

Jedidah stood completely still—rigid and white-faced. Huldah rushed to her and led her to the couch. "Sit here."

Wailing and sobbing, the princess cried out, "No, no, no! He mustn't do that to Josiah." She put one arm around her son and pressed his head against her breast.

Huldah leaned down and whispered, "Shallum knows, and he has a plan."

"A plan? What plan?"

"He can take Josiah to someone he trusts in a town north of Jerusalem."

Jedidah lifted the sleeve of her tunic to wipe away her tears. "Yes, he must take him. Tell Shallum to take him tonight, otherwise it might be too late. When you go to teach your class, ask Miriama to come here. I need her help."

Huldah reached out to pat Josiah's back, and then reluctantly left the room.

After delivering the message to Miriama, she toiled through the lesson with the ladies of the court. At the same time her mind raced ahead to the unknown consequences of Shallum's plan. Could he smuggle the little boy out of the palace and slip past numerous guards? Could he outdistance pursuers all the way to Anathoth or the eastern lands? Would she ever again see the child she loved . . . or the man she wanted to marry?

A subdued Miriama led her to the gate where Shallum waited. On the way to her father's house, he did not speak, but after they entered the courtyard, he pulled her into his arms. Holding her to him, with his head touching hers, he whispered, "I'll take Josiah tonight."

For a long moment Huldah clung to him before she could let him go. After the gate closed behind him, she listened to his fading footsteps. To avoid the chatter of her mother and Kezia in the kitchen, she retreated to the quietness of her room.

Sometime during the night a loud knocking awakened her. She heard her father walk across the courtyard and speak to the watchmen he had hired to guard his gate. "What's the matter out there?"

"There's a woman here who says she has a message for you."

"At this time of night?"

"Please, let me in," the woman pleaded.

Recognizing Miriama's voice, Huldah left her room and ran to her father. "It's Shallum's sister."

He unbarred the gate. As soon as Miriama hurried in, Huldah put her arm around the young woman's trembling shoulders.

"What's this all about?" Barak demanded.

Between deep sobs, words came. "The plan failed. Guards caught Shallum with Josiah. They've taken my brother to the dungeon, and Amon grabbed his son and has hidden him somewhere in the palace. Jedidah doesn't know where."

"Oh, no!" cried Huldah.

"Speak quietly, you two," ordered Barak. "This is threatening information."

"You are right, my lord," replied Miriama politely. "It's dangerous for me to relate this information and for you to hear it. But I must tell you more. Prince Amon says that if Huldah returns to the palace or even walks in the city streets, he will have his soldiers arrest her and . . ."

"And?" prompted Barak.

". . . and execute her."

"Stupid, incompetent fool," growled Huldah's father. "When will we ever have an end to all these depraved times in Judah?"

Miriama adjusted her shawl to cover most of her face. "I must hurry back to the princess."

Huldah hugged her. "How will you get into the palace again?"

"I know a way. There's a captain of the guard who will help me."

"Go then," said Barak, "and may God go with you." The remainder of that night Huldah lay awake. Too many questions pressed down upon her. Would Amon order his soldiers to take Shallum out to the Hinnom Valley and strike him down? Or would the prince throw him in a damp dungeon and leave him without enough food and water until he wasted away? Or was Amon perhaps planning an elaborate execution as part of Manasseh's homecoming celebration? And where was Josiah? She pictured the two-year-old boy, locked in a box, frightened, and crying for his mother. *And I can't even go to the princess to sympathize with her*, thought Huldah. *I'm a prisoner in my father's house.*

The days passed slowly. Each morning she walked in the courtyard. Coriander growing in pots showed its lacy white blossoms. Thyme produced a display of tiny lavender flowers. In the kitchen she shaped bread dough into loaves. In her room she tried to concentrate on reading. She spoke little to her parents and Kezia, and they in turn

54

respected her grief over Shallum and Josiah.

Autumn arrived, then winter. Every day old Samuel ventured out to the marketplace, where he listened for news and gossip. Although travelers arrived from the north, they carried no reports about when the king of Assyria would release Manasseh. Then one morning when Samuel returned from his daily trip, he was hardly inside the courtyard wall before he announced, "Big excitement. Our king and a remnant of the men captured with him are a two-day's journey from Jerusalem."

Huldah ran to her room and threw herself onto the bed. The time for Amon's big celebration had come. Now he would offer Josiah as a burnt offering to Molech. Now . . . Shallum. Sobs ripped from her throat.

Two days later many of the citizens waited in the streets for the return of their king—not out of love but out of curiosity. Amon, dressed in his most elaborate robe and jewelry, marched out with an honor guard of a thousand men to meet his father.

That afternoon Huldah was surprised to see Barak come home early. He seated himself on a bench in the courtyard and shook his head. "It's hard to believe. I hope it's true."

She stood in front of him. "What's hard to believe?"

"I was there and heard it myself. King Manasseh entered the city and climbed up a stairway onto the city wall. There he proclaimed in a loud voice that when he was in prison, he repented of his sinful ways and asked the Lord to render his enemies merciful. In answer to his prayers, the Assyrians released him, and God brought him to Jerusalem. In return Manasseh will worship only the one true God. He will allow no sacrifices to Baal or Molech or any other foreign idol."

"That means Josiah is safe!" exclaimed Huldah. "But do

you think the king will release Shallum?"

"We must not give up hope."

All the next day she listened to footsteps in the street, but none were the ones she wanted to hear. The second morning a winter rain blew in from the west. She huddled by her hearth, shelling dried red lentils for barley and lentil porridge. Raindrops pounded onto the courtyard stones, drowning out any sound from the street. When Samuel's cracking voice announced, "A guest is here," Huldah raised her head in surprise. Shallum stood inside the gate, water running off his heavy woolen cloak.

She ran to him and pulled him to the warmth of the kitchen hearth. "Let me hang up your cloak by the fire." He removed it, and she hung it onto wooden pegs that projected from the wall.

When she turned around, Shallum held out his hands to her, "Josiah is with his mother again."

"Thanks to God," said Huldah. His hands were cold in her warm ones, and his cheek felt cool against hers. When she put her arms around him, she could feel the thinness of his body through his robe and tunic. "You lost weight while you were in that dungeon."

"Some days I had only a handful of parched wheat to eat, other days a small loaf of barley bread."

"I've been so worried about you and waited so long to see you."

"Yesterday I had business to attend to."

Of *course*, she thought as she drew herself out of his embrace, *he has more important business than coming to see me. I must always remember that he is a nobleman working for the king.*

Chapter 7

Yesterday," he continued, "I bought a house." So that was his business—a house. Huldah clasped her hands together in delight. "Does that mean we can set a new date for our wedding?"

He grinned at her. "After I leave here I'll go to the scribes' quarters to talk to your father about the marriage feast."

The exciting thought sent a fluttering to her heart. Smiling, she asked, "Where is the house?"

"In the second quarter, the new section that King Hezekiah built shortly before he died."

"Near the Temple mount?"

"Yes. And I've also hired the servants—two cooks and three maidservants for you, two menservants for me, and, of course, a doorkeeper for inside and guards for outside the gate."

Huldah's smile faded. "Do we need so many?" He cupped her face in his hands. "I want you to have all the help you need. The house has numerous rooms and a large banquet hall. King Manasseh has promoted me to become chief keeper of his wardrobe, and with this new position, I'll need to entertain guests in our home." His gentle kiss gave her hope that she could live up to his expectations. He took his cloak from the wall. "I'll go now to see your father."

The smell of warm wool from his cloak lingered in the kitchen. Huldah stared into the fire . . . chief keeper of the king's wardrobe . . . a large house, many servants, a banquet room for important guests . . . the duties of a nobleman's wife.

* * *

King Manasseh lost no time in implementing his reforms. He ordered his servants to take all the images and altars of idols from the Temple mount and throw them into the Hinnom Valley. He hired workers to strengthen the city's fortifications, to repair the walls, build towers, and construct an outer wall around the west and north sides of Jerusalem. In the Temple the priests restored the Lord's altar and offered sacrifices of peace and thanksgiving. "In all of Judah," Manasseh commanded, "we will serve only the one true God."

* * *

"Your father has agreed to a marriage feast at the second new moon," Shallum announced to Huldah. "This will give me time to prepare our home."

"And for my preparations . . ." she answered with thoughts racing ahead to packing clothes and her most priceless possessions—her scrolls.

Abital and Kezia plunged into activity—plans for the

feast, shopping for supplies. Along with Barak and the bride-to-be they accepted Shallum's invitation to inspect his house. Surveying the banquet room, Abital nodded her approval. "Nice and big. Just the right size for a wedding feast."

Kezia added her opinions. "The kitchen is large enough to roast the lambs."

After wandering in and out of the rooms, Huldah stood with Shallum in the courtyard. "I didn't realize the house was so large, and it even has its own cistern."

He squeezed her hand. "I wanted to give you a pleasant surprise."

On the wedding day, Miriama appeared at Barak's house to help dress the bride. In Huldah's room, the two young women gazed at each other. "You probably have wondered why I talked so much about Shallum," Miriama said. "From the first time I saw you, I felt you were the woman for him."

Huldah touched Miriama's hand. "Thank you. I've never had a sister. Now I have you."

"And I have you." She laughed happily. "May I help prepare my new sister for the wedding feast?"

In their newfound friendship, Miriama confided that she was in love with Enosh, a captain of the king's guard, and Huldah confessed her concern about marrying into a family of noble birth.

"You may not have been born into such a family, but I think you're truly as noble as my brother or I." She glanced around the room. "Now where's your wedding gown?"

Huldah removed it from an acacia-wood chest. Miriama unfolded the clean, white goat's wool set off with elaborate blue, yellow, and red embroidery. "It's lovely."

Stroking the soft fabric, the bride added, "I've waited a long time to wear it."

Later in the day Miriama opened a box. "I brought my strings of pearls and turquoise to adorn your hair. We want you to look like a queen." Along with the jewels, she fashioned Huldah's brown hair into thick braids. She placed the golden betrothal necklace around the bride's neck and draped the embroidered woolen shawl over her head.

At dusk all preparations were complete. Abital and Kezia returned from Shallum's house where they had supervised the roasting of lambs for the feast. Dressed in fine robes, the family waited for the groom to arrive. Even the doorkeeper Samuel wore a new cloak.

"For lo, the winter is past, the rain is over and gone," Huldah quoted from one of her scrolls. "The flowers appear on the earth, the time of singing has come, and the voice of the turtledove is heard in our land."

"That's beautiful," sighed Miriama.

"The turtledoves remind me of the night that Shallum and I carried Josiah to the Temple mount. I wish I could see that little boy at my wedding."

"It cannot happen. Prince Amon has refused to allow the princess to attend, but the ladies of the court will come."

At the sound of singing in the street, Miriama fastened a veil over Huldah's face. Shallum's voice rang out, "Open for Shallum, son of Tikvah. I have come for my bride, Huldah, daughter of Barak."

Samuel had the honor of opening the gate for the groom and the group of men with him. Huldah's father led her to him and placed her hand in his. Barak removed the veil that covered his daughter's face and placed the veil on Shallum's shoulder. Then he declared the traditional words, "The government of his household shall be upon his shoulder." The guests shouted their approval, drowning out the sounds of Abital's and Kezia's joyful sobs.

Huldah held tightly to Shallum's arm, needing support for the excitement that caused her knees to feel weak. Without her veil, she could see that he was dressed as a king. He had gained weight, and the ornate robe fit well. On his head he wore a golden crown, and in his hand he carried another. When he placed it on Huldah's head, the guests renewed their shouting.

Barak's voice carried above the boisterous congratulations. "Let the procession begin." As he strode out the gate, the bridal couple followed behind him, and the guests trailed along. Abital, Kezia, and Miriama walked together. Each person carried a small clay lamp with a single wick burning in olive oil. The men sang a lively melody, and from somewhere in the street ahead, women's voices joined the song. As the procession turned down a side street, Huldah saw the ladies of the court. Light from their lamps illuminated the passageway.

In the banquet room of the new house, Huldah and Shallum sat under a canopy of green cypress boughs and fragrant spring flowers. During the leisurely meal, Huldah took her place as queen of the feast and, along with Shallum, responded regally to the guests' benedictions and her father's blessing: "May you increase to thousands upon thousands; may your offspring possess the gates of their enemies."

Late in the night the ladies of the court ushered the bride to a richly decorated bedchamber. Soon the groom's friends brought him. Alone together in the room, Shallum slowly lifted the crown from his head and gave it to Huldah. In turn she removed hers and handed it to him. They placed their crowns side by side on a table, and she stepped closer to him. His arms encircled her, and her heart sang, I'm married to the man I love.

* * *

The feasting continued for seven days, and then Huldah became mistress of her household, learning to deal with the servants and the large number of rooms. At the proper time, 30 days after the wedding, she returned to the palace. No longer needing an escort now that she was married, she walked alone through the streets. When she entered the women's garden, she heard a squeal of laughter. Josiah raced down a path and into her arms. The Egyptian dog joined in, leaping and barking a welcome. Huldah hugged the little boy and patted the hound. Miriama greeted her, "The princess is waiting for you." They left Josiah under the watchful care of three maidservants.

Before they entered Jedidah's chambers, a Nubian slave addressed Huldah. "King Manasseh knows that you are here and he requests your presence."

"Me?" She grabbed Miriama's hand. "Why would he want to see me?"

Miriama's eyes were wide with alarm. "I don't know, but you'll have to do as he orders."

Reluctantly Huldah let go of her sister-in-law's hand. Taking a deep breath, she followed the slave through a long passageway to a heavy door. The door opened and two soldiers ushered her into a wider hall and down stone steps to the royal buildings where the monarch conducted business. Shivering from the unheated corridors and deep apprehension, Huldah waited while the soldiers announced her arrival. She heard the king's voice. "Let the woman enter."

Expecting to see a dazzling room with ornate tapestries and ivory throne, she stared in surprise at the small chamber. The king, dressed in a plain white robe, stood near a window. "Are you Huldah, wife of Shallum, the keeper of my wardrobe?"

"Yes, my lord."

"Do you teach the ladies of the court to read?"

Will he condemn me to a dungeon for teaching without his permission?

Faintly she answered, "Yes, my lord."

"From now on I want you to enlarge your school to include the wives and daughters of my captains and city officials."

Huldah blinked in relief, and a great joy surged through her. She could teach even more women to read.

Manasseh motioned to a window that opened to the south. "Come over here." In a confusion of awe she stepped to the window, where the king pointed down to the wall of the building.

"See those gates that lead into the royal court and the palace? I will send out a proclamation that certain women shall attend your school, and I will instruct my guards to allow them through those gates." He turned away from the window, "From now on you will no longer use Sumerian writings. You will teach the history of our people, using scrolls that I keep in my library."

"Thank you, my lord."

In the passageways, Huldah walked with her head up and a smile on her lips. *My school! I can teach from Hebrew scrolls—the prophecies of Isaiah and history from our chronicles.*

*   *   *

In the months that followed, Huldah greeted each day in happy anticipation of satisfying hours with her students. The school flourished. Women from the city came to learn, and the court ladies continued their studies.

With Manasseh's reforms and the hiring of workmen to repair the city's old walls and build new ones, prosperity returned to Jerusalem. Trade with other countries increased, benefiting all of Judah. Priests in the Temple sacrificed only to the one true God.

In an appropriate celebration, Miriama married Enosh, the captain of the guards, and during the next two years she produced a daughter and then a son.

But for Huldah and Shallum no babies arrived. "My happiness would be complete," she told her husband, "If I could give you a son."

In the cool of a summer evening, they were sitting on the roof of their home. From here they could see the dark outline of Solomon's Temple against light that lingered in the sky. A meaty smell of smoke from the last of the day's sacrifices drifted in the still air.

"I, too, long for a son," Shallum answered, "but if God chooses not to send one, we must accept His judgment." After a moment he added, "Often I think of Josiah as our son. The princess is generous to share him with us."

"Yes, she is, and she's told me that Prince Amon doesn't know how close we are to his son."

"It's safer if he doesn't know." Shallum shook his head. "It seems only a short time ago that we took Josiah to the priest for redemption, and now he's already five years old. The court scribe says Josiah reads well for his age."

"Yes, sometimes he reads to me. He's a bright child. That's just as well since he'll soon become king."

Shallum shifted on his chair and leaned toward her. "What makes you think he will soon become king?"

"I don't know. It's just a feeling I have."

He laid his hand on her arm. "You've mentioned other events before they happened. Do you think God's given you a gift? Might He have given you the ability to prophesy?"

"Oh! I don't think so." Huldah shrank back against her chair. "If that was true, what would the Lord expect of me?"

Chapter 8

He would expect you to interpret his messages for the people."

"But most prophets are men," Huldah protested.

Shallum's voice was gentle, yet firm. "Not all. Don't forget Deborah—and Moses' sister, Miriama. If God has chosen you to receive His gift of interpreting messages, you must accept it."

She gazed down at the rooftop and shook her head, "I'm not good enough."

"No one's good enough. Even Moses' sister displeased the Lord for awhile, but he forgave her."

Reaching for the comfort of her husband's hand, she fretted, "I wouldn't know how to begin."

"You've always trusted in the Lord. I'm sure He'll tell you what to do."

"I have trusted, but He's never asked me to do something so hard."

As the days passed, the idea that she possessed the

gift of prophecy seldom left Huldah's mind. *Has the Lord really chosen me to serve in this way?* she wondered. *If so, am I capable of using His gift to interpret messages? When would He expect me to begin?*

One morning while Huldah was teaching the ladies, a maidservant timidly entered the room.

"Why are you here?" Miriama asked.

"King Manasseh has sent a message," the woman answered. "He requests the presence of the teacher."

A shiver passed through Huldah. *Why has the king called me again? Have I displeased him in some way?* She followed the servant out of the room and down the long halls and passageways to the royal courts. This time the king waited for her in his ornate reception room. Golden tapestries covered the walls, and he sat on an ivory throne. Numerous courtiers stood behind and to the sides of him. Court scribes sat at tables. Before Huldah bowed her head to the king, she caught a glimpse of her husband standing among the men.

"Huldah, wife of Shallum," Manasseh greeted her, "I have made a decision about you."

She clasped her hands together to control their trembling. "Yes, my lord."

"I know that you have studied our history and the writings of our prophets. Men as well as women could benefit from your counsel. Therefore I ordered workmen to prepare a room for you in the marketplace at the city center. It is now ready, and you will sit there three days of each week to receive any person who wishes to inquire about messages from God."

"Yes, my lord," Huldah gasped her polite response, but without thinking more words tumbled out, "You want me to interpret God's messages?"

"Wait!" Prince Amon pushed his way through the

courtiers and stood between his father and Huldah. "No woman should sit in the center of the city and act like some sort of prophet. It's not right for any woman, especially this one who is married to that traitor Shallum."

The king stood up. "I have spoken, and I repeat that this woman will sit in the center of the city and receive any person who wishes to inquire about God's messages. Her presence there will show the people that I believe in the Lord's guidance." He looked directly at his son. "My soldiers will guard her." Turning to Huldah he said, "I dismiss you to your duties."

Agonizing over Amon's hostility to Shallum, she backed out of the room and into the passageway. As she hurried toward the women's quarters, familiar footsteps sounded behind her. Stopping at a window that overlooked a garden, she waited for her husband. "I'll have soldiers to guard me," she blurted, "but you won't have them to protect you from Prince Amon."

"As long as King Manasseh is alive," he assured her, "I have nothing to worry about."

She pressed her face against his shoulder but could not speak.

The next morning Huldah got up early to choose which scroll to carry with her to the marketplace. Spreading several on her table, she considered them carefully. *In case I need to find answers in a prophet's writings*, she decided, *I'll take Isaiah's.*

Before Shallum left for his work at the palace, he held her in his steady embrace. "With the Lord's help, you'll do well."

"Without His help, I could never interpret His messages."

When two soldiers arrived to escort her to the city center, she was ready. One soldier walked in front and one followed as they paraded her through the familiar streets. Shoppers on their way to market paused to stare at Huldah and her escorts.

With a start she realized the soldiers were heading away from the marketplace. She hurried to catch up with the guard in front of her. "Where are you taking me?"

"To the scribes' quarters."

"Why?"

"King Manasseh's orders. He wants the scribes to see you on your way to the marketplace."

To the scribes' quarters! Although she had sent a message to her parents telling them about her assignment, what would her father think if the soldiers paraded her through his place of business?

The street entered the scribes' quarters through an archway and ran the length of the long building. On both sides of the indoor street, scribes sat on platforms. Low, wooden walls divided the platforms into stalls for each man's designated place. Large windows and unroofed sections of the building let in sufficient light for the scribes to see while using their writing reeds and ink on papyrus.

Clients were already arriving to seek help in conducting the day's business, and a confusion of voices echoed throughout the working place.

Probably the people here think the soldiers have arrested me, Huldah fretted, *and are marching me around the city as a bad example before taking me to prison.*

Some men frowned at her, others shook their heads. Her father's place lay at the far end. She saw him standing near his table, and when close enough, she was relieved to see him smiling at her. All too quickly the soldiers hurried her past.

Out of the building, she soon heard the usual sounds from the marketplace where vendors called out their wares to shoppers. Their voices grew louder as the soldiers guided her through a narrow street to the market's open section. Here the sides of the street broadened to form a wide area where vendors sold food, and peddlers spread their goods on the stones. At one side, walls of a new mud-brick booth supported a wooden roof. The lead soldier pointed to the booth. "This is the place the king ordered for you." Leaving her there, the guards wandered across the market area to a seller of almonds and dates.

Through the booth's open front, Huldah saw a small table and two benches. She stepped up to the stone floor and placed the scroll on the table. What if no one came? Would anyone want to inquire of a woman prophet? Unrolling the papyrus, she sat down to read from the words of Isaiah. "Trust in the Lord forever, for the Lord God is an everlasting Rock."

Looking up from her reading, she saw two little boys in ragged robes standing by her step. "What are you going to sell?" the smaller boy asked.

She found the boys and their eager question appealing. "I'm not going to sell anything. King Manasseh said that I would sit here to answer questions anyone has about God's messages."

"Has anyone asked a question?"

"Not yet."

The older boy's face brightened. "We'll go find someone for you." And they dashed away.

Huldah smiled at their exuberance but doubted they would find someone to bring.

Across the way the soldiers were munching on dates and almonds while they chatted with an attractive young woman. Near them a baker checked the fire in his large oven. Huldah could see round loaves of unbaked bread on a table inside the man's stall. Next to him a grain merchant was measuring wheat and pouring it into a tightly-woven basket for a servant woman. A donkey loaded with leather passed the stalls, and its driver directed the animal toward the sandalmakers' street.

On one side of Huldah's booth, a spice merchant's shop gave forth the aroma of sweet basil and spicy cinnamon. On the other side, a fruit vendor called to passing shoppers, "Pomegranates. Ripe, red pomegranates, ready to eat."

A man approached Huldah's stall. "Father!" she exclaimed in happy surprise.

A proud expression crossed his face. "Just now the crier of daily news passed through the scribes' quarters and announced that the prophetess Huldah was seated in the marketplace. I have come to welcome you to the center of the city."

"Thank you, Father, but do you think anyone will come to ask for my counsel?"

He glanced behind him. "I see two little boys directing a man this way."

She bit her lip and wiped her perspiring hands on the sleeves of her robe. "I'm ready."

The man stepped up and seated himself on the opposite bench. "The crier of daily news said that a prophetess in the marketplace could answer questions about the worship of God. I have come for some answers."

Huldah took a deep breath and silently prayed, *Help me, Lord.*

* * *

Before long, she settled into a routine of counseling those who asked about God's messages, teaching the women, and reading with Josiah. She and Shallum lived

71

comfortably in their home, only now and then mentioning the apprehension that lay close to the surface in their thoughts—dread of the time when Amon might begin his reign.

It was on a hazy autumn day that King Manasseh suddenly became ill. By the next morning he was dead. Cries and wailing filled the streets as the period of lamentation began for the king.

That day the soldiers did not arrive to escort Huldah to her place in the city center.

"I have to go to the palace and choose the proper robe for the king's burial," Shallum told her.

"No, you mustn't. It's not safe for you."

"It may not be safe, but it's still my duty." After he left, Huldah wandered from room to room, trying to stay out of the way of the maidservants, who were scrubbing the floors and sweeping the courtyard. She was in the kitchen conferring with the cooks when she heard a call at the gate.

When the doorkeeper opened for her, Miriama stumbled into the courtyard and dropped onto a bench. "It's happened again," she sobbed. "They've taken Shallum to the dungeon."

Huldah held her hands over her face and sank onto the bench next to her sister-in-law. "Oh, no. He shouldn't have gone to the palace this morning."

Miriama put her arm around Huldah's shoulders. "They would have come here to get him."

"What will they do to him?"

"I don't know, but Enosh says that when he's on duty, he'll make sure none of his guards mistreat Shallum. He also told me to advise you to remain inside your house. You're safer here." Quickly she hugged Huldah and then stood up. "I'm sorry I can't stay longer."

"You'll come whenever there's news, won't you?"

"Whenever I can."

Alone again in the courtyard Huldah sat on the bench in stunned silence. *In prison, in prison, my husband is in prison*, echoed through her mind. "How long, Lord," she begged to know, "How long can we expect our new king to give these cruel orders?"

His father had reigned for 55 years. But in a shorter time Amon could bring about more corruption than Manasseh had before the Assyrians captured him.

To the citizens of Jerusalem, Amon announced, "My father was a strong man before he went into captivity. I will rule as he did at that time. I will provide altars for Baal and set up asherim—the wooden pillars for Asherah, goddess of fertility." Soon workmen retrieved the idols that Manasseh had thrown into the Hinnom Valley. They hauled them to the mount and set them in the courtyard and in the Temple.

Once again a prisoner in her house, Huldah fought against the deep worry that threatened to overwhelm her. She longed to see her husband, to hear his footsteps arriving home, to feel his arms around her. Without enough food, was he growing thin and weaker each day? She wished she could carry provisions to him—almonds, dried apricots, a loaf of wheat bread.

Miriama brought news. "Whenever he can, Enosh smuggles extra food to Shallum."

Huldah squeezed her sister-in-law's hand. "Tell your husband that I'm grateful."

A note of despair crept into Miriama's voice. "King Amon pays tribute to the Assyrians, and he's doing all in his power to please them. He has ordered worship of all the pagan idols, not just Baal and Asherah."

"Even . . . even Molech?"

"Even Molech. Some of the courtiers are against

Amon's concessions to the Assyrians and worship of idols, but they are afraid to criticize him. Poor Jedidah is living in fear that her husband will sacrifice Josiah to Molech."

Huldah gave a deep groan. "How *is* the little boy?"

Miriama shook her head. "He's terrified of his father. Whenever Amon comes, Josiah runs to hide."

* * *

As the months passed, Huldah's father and mother came daily to visit her. "I wish you were home with us," complained Abital, "instead of here in this big house."

"This is my home," Huldah answered. "I'll wait here for Shallum to return."

"Who knows when that will happen?" grumbled Barak. "Trade has fallen off again. With no building going on, workmen are idle. More and more of the poor are homeless and hungry. Thieves enter houses or rob people in the streets—I knew this would happen when Amon became king."

After they returned to their house, Huldah settled in front of her hearth. She picked up her embroidery, a large woolen wall hanging she was fashioning for her husband's room. It covered her knees and spread onto the carpeted floor. The wool's warmth felt good on this late autumn day. *Two years already*, she mused. *Two years since Shallum left our home to choose a robe for King Manasseh's burial.*

A gust of wind blew against the wall and whined through a crack. Soon rain spattered against the house.

Early the next morning shouts in the street awakened her. Leaving her room she encountered her servants clustered in the damp courtyard, and she instructed the doorkeeper to find out the reason for the noise. He soon returned, trembling with excitement. "King Amon is dead.

Last night some of his courtiers attacked him with daggers."

"Oh," screamed a maidservant, "no one is safe, not even a king."

"You're right," agreed the doorkeeper. "A mob of citizens is marching right now toward the palace. Rumor is that they want to make sure those men of the court don't kill the entire royal family and other nobles and then seize the power to rule with a new royal line."

"Don't anyone leave this house," advised Huldah. "Here you are safer than in the streets." She returned to her room so they wouldn't see the tears that were seeping into her eyes. Prince Josiah and his little brother. . . Queen Jedidah . . . Miriama . . . Shallum. Danger threatened all of them.

The tears overflowed. "Lord, if only I could talk to Shallum . . ." In sudden illogical determination she reached for her woolen cloak. "I'll go. Yes, I'll go to the palace, and I'll search until I find my husband."

Chapter 9

Ignoring her own better judgment and oblivious to the disapproval of her doorkeeper and warnings from the guards outside the gate, Huldah left the courtyard and headed toward the palace. As she wound through the deserted streets, she became aware of the strange quiet. Only the sound of her sandals on the stones broke the stillness. No shouts filled the marketplace. Merchants had barred the doors of their shops and retreated behind the walls. Her mind raced ahead. *First I'll look for Miriama, and she'll tell me how to find Shallum.*

At the approach to the palace, Huldah paused in shock when she spotted only a few soldiers looking down from the walls. Entering the courtyard, she hurried to the women's garden and found the two Nubians still guarding the entry to the women's quarters. Surprise showed on their faces. "We thought you might never return to the palace," one of them said.

After they allowed her into the building, she ran through the hallway and up the staircase to Jedidah's door.

Without waiting for an invitation, she burst into the reception room.

The queen stood by the window with her hands to the sides of her face. "Huldah! They killed Amon. His courtiers, the ones he trusted. They've seized power and I'm afraid they'll come for my sons."

Huldah drew her to a couch and sat with her arm around the terrified woman. "Where are the boys?"

"I've hidden them in my bedchamber." Jedidah pressed her fists against her eyes. "Amon was only 24 years old. I hoped the Lord would speak to him and change him like He changed his father. Two years was not enough time. Now my hope is gone." She bowed her head and strands of dark hair fell across her face.

Tears came to Huldah's eyes, not for Amon but for her friend.

From somewhere outside the palace, angry shouting rose and fell. Jedidah raised her head. "You must leave immediately. It's not safe for you here. Now that the courtiers have seized power, they'll break into the women's quarters to rid themselves of all the royal family and our servants. There's no need for you to lose your life just because you're my friend. They'll search the women's quarters until they find us."

"What about the secret room beneath the floor? Can't we all hide there?"

"The courtiers know about the room. It's the first place they'd look," Jedidah wailed. "I can't bear to think of what they'll do to my sons."

Huldah walked to the window and peered down into a courtyard but saw no one there. As she searched past the wall to a hillside, the sounds began to recede. Returning to Jedidah, she sat in silence next to the queen. *If only I could find Shallum. He would know what to do.*

Without warning Miriama dashed into the room. "Do you hear all the noise? A mob of citizens overcame the guards at the royal court. They broke down the gates and entered the building. Now they've captured some of the courtiers and are taking them to the Hinnom Valley for execution."

The queen let out a deep breath and lay down on the couch. "All this killing," she moaned. "Now that the citizens have seized power, what will happen next?"

Huldah turned to Miriama and asked anxiously, "Do you have any news of Shallum? I came to find him, but I don't know how."

"I haven't been able to learn anything about him." Miriama replied nervously. "No one responds to my call at the doors to the men's quarters. I don't know what's happened to either my brother or my husband, but I'll keep on trying to find them." After a troubled glance at the prostrate queen, she hurried out.

The door to Jedidah's inner chambers banged open, and Josiah ran into the room. "What's going on? The servants won't tell me anything."

He had grown taller during the two years Huldah had remained in her home. Black hair curled around his ears. His dark brown eyes showed the same apprehension that sounded in his voice.

"You tell him," whispered Jedidah.

"Your father . . . " Huldah began but stopped, not knowing how to relate the news that the boy's father was dead.

Josiah came across the room to stand close to her. "Huldah, I haven't seen you for a long, long time." He looked directly into her eyes. "Did something happen to my father?"

There was no way she could keep the frightening news

from him. "Yes. Some of the courtiers have taken his life."

A frown creased his forehead. "Mother told me that some day he might become a good king, but I guess it's too late for that." He paused before whispering, "I was afraid of him, but I didn't want him to die."

"None of us expected him to die."

Josiah's face took on a look of concentration. "Since my father is no longer king, does that mean that I have to become king right away?"

Wanting to hold him in her arms as she had when he was younger, Huldah restrained herself. She took his hand in hers. "That's the way it usually happens."

Jedidah sat up. "But it might not happen that way this time. We don't know what that mob of citizens will do. Huldah, you must disguise my sons and take them away. Anywhere. Away."

Before Huldah could answer, the door opened and Miriama entered again. "Some of the citizens have returned from the valley, and they're asking to see Josiah."

His mother stood up. "Hide him somewhere. I don't want to lose my son."

"No, they won't harm Josiah. The people are ready to proclaim him the new king."

At that moment noise erupted in the passageway, and someone flung open the door. A large man in a blood-stained robe stepped into the room. "Josiah is king! We've come to take him to the royal court and declare that he is king." A group of men shoved in behind him, and others in the hallway crowded toward them.

Wide-eyed, the boy looked toward his mother. She left her place by the couch and, taking a deep breath, stood composed and regal to face the men. "You will crown my son Josiah in the proper and traditional manner with a priest of the Lord to anoint him."

Astonished, the citizens stared at the slender young queen confronting them. One man found enough courage to speak. "Of course our intentions were honorable, but we transgressed when we invaded your quarters. We will go to the high priest and arrange the proper coronation ceremony for our next king." The men backed out of the room and shouted to the waiting crowd, "To the Temple mount. We must talk to the high priest."

Having spent her energy, Jedidah drooped again onto the couch. From the inner chambers another dark-haired boy, younger than his brother Josiah, raced into the room and scrambled onto the couch next to his mother. He hid his face against her arm.

Josiah stood in front of Jedidah. "As soon as I am king, I'm going to order happy times for everyone."

Running footsteps again sounded in the hallway, and Miriama burst into the room. "I found Enosh, and he told me the guards had released all prisoners. Shallum might be on his way home."

Huldah turned to face the queen. "Then may I leave to go to my husband?"

With her younger son on the couch and Josiah standing by her side, Jedidah spoke softly, "You are dismissed. I still have my two sons to give me comfort."

An uneasy quiet hovered over the streets of Jerusalem. Still wary of mob violence, only a few men and women ventured out of their homes.

As Huldah walked briskly along the nearly deserted streets, her heart beat more rapidly when she thought that Shallum might have arrived home and was waiting for her. Or after two years in the dungeon was he too sick to walk? Could he make it safely through the streets?

Watching for any glimpse of her husband crumpled in a doorway or against a wall, she finally reached their own gate. A manservant opened it for her, and she rushed into the courtyard. "Has the master of the house arrived?"

Smiling, the servant pointed to Shallum's room, "He's there."

As Huldah hurried across the courtyard, a pale man with an unkempt gray beard stepped out of the room. When he limped forward, she realized it was Shallum. Abruptly she stopped to stare at him. He reached out to her with thin hands, and she stepped toward him until his arms encircled her. "Shallum, Shallum," she whispered.

His voice was low and husky. "The servants said you went to look for me."

"And I've found you in our own home." Huldah placed her arm around his waist and steered him into the warmth of his room. "I was afraid that if either the courtiers or the people of the city took you, I'd never see you again." She pressed her head against his shoulder, and her tears spilled onto his musty, ragged robe. "What did they do to you in that prison? You're so thin and you're limping."

He held her close. "Two years in a dungeon takes away strength, but now that I'm home with you, I'll recover."

"Yes, you're home," she whispered, thinking that after two years of days and nights without him, now she was home again in his arms. She lifted her head from his shoulder and waited for his kiss. It came soft and gentle on her waiting lips. Then he smiled down at her and kissed her again, more eagerly this time.

When knocking sounded at the gate and a servant crossed the courtyard to open it, Shallum's body tensed and he stared suspiciously into the courtyard. Seeing only their doorkeeper enter, he left the room to talk to the man. "What's the latest news?"

The doorkeeper's face brightened into a broad smile. "Welcome home, Master Shallum. I learned in the streets that the citizens released you from prison."

"Tell me the news," demanded Shallum. "What about these citizens? Have they returned to their homes?"

The doorkeeper shook his head. "Not yet. They're up on the Temple mount conferring with the high priest Hilkiah."

"What business have they with Hilkiah?"

"They're asking him to proclaim Josiah as king."

Turning to Huldah who was standing behind him, Shallum asked, "Soldiers would tell me nothing, but people in the streets said that Amon is dead. Is this true?"

"It's true," she replied and then watched her husband silently ponder the news.

At last he spoke. "Josiah is only eight years old. There are always groups of citizens or nobles or priests who would like to seize power for themselves. Can we trust anyone? Outside enemies will hear about Judah's boy king and consider this a good time to invade. Who will come first? Assyrians, Babylonians, Chaldeans, or Egyptians?" He limped to the door of his room. "As soon as I'm able, I'll go to the royal court and offer my services to Josiah."

The doorkeeper entered the menservants' quarters, and Huldah stood alone in the courtyard.

"Can we trust anyone?" she repeated. Remembering the young queen facing the mob of citizens, Huldah felt confident that from his mother's side of the family, strong blood flowed in Josiah's veins. She would trust the righteousness that Jedidah had already imparted and would continue to inspire in the boy king.

But he was still only a little boy with designing men—some unscrupulous and crafty—surrounding him. Huldah looked up at the gloomy winter sky. "Lord God, she prayed, "guard this child and the great task that lies ahead of him."

Two days later dressed in a clean robe and with his gray beard neatly trimmed, Shallum announced, "Today I will go to the royal court."

Eager to see Josiah, Huldah asked, "May I go with you?"

As they strolled through the streets, Shallum reached for his wife's hand. "This is like the old times when I escorted you to the palace."

She smiled in remembrance, and yet a feeling of uneasiness crept over her. The city remained too quiet, and she noticed that only a few shoppers headed toward the marketplace. She looked up at the sky. A westerly wind blowing somber clouds suggested the return of rain.

They entered through one of the southern gates and made their way up to the royal court. Miriama's husband, Enosh, stood guard outside the king's reception room. "Many officials are waiting to speak to Josiah, but I'll let you in next. He's been asking for you."

He rapped with the hilt of his sword on the door. When a soldier cautiously opened it, Huldah's gaze was drawn immediately to the boy seated on the high ivory throne. A wave of concern washed over her. Josiah leaned against silken cushions and appeared tired. How small he looked on that big throne with his feet dangling above the floor.

Scribes sat at tables, and courtiers clustered on both sides of the throne. Hilkiah, the high priest, stood near the king. Some of the courtiers whispered among themselves and glanced distrustfully at Shallum.

Chapter 10

When he saw his visitors, Josiah's eyes brightened and he sat up straighter.

Shallum was the first to speak. "I have come to offer my services to our new king."

A smile livened the boy's face. "That's good." He leaned toward the high priest, and they conferred for a few moments. "Hilkiah is my advisor," Josiah explained. "We think you should be the keeper of my wardrobe just like you were for my grandfather."

Shallum bowed to the young king. "The honor is mine."

Josiah's gaze rested on Huldah. "I want you to come to the palace too."

She bowed her head and offered, "I could open my school for the ladies again."

Hilkiah spoke with Josiah. The boy turned to Huldah. "My advisor thinks you should teach in the palace and also sit at the city center to interpret messages from the Lord. That's what I want you to do." He slipped off the throne and stood looking up at the priest. "And right now I want to go to the garden and play with my dog."

The courtier Zophar stepped forward. "But, my lord, many officials are waiting to see you."

Hilkiah faced him. "I have anointed Josiah as king. If he wishes to go to the garden to play with his dog, he may go."

Josiah marched to the door and ordered the doorkeepers to open it. Before leaving he turned around. "Shallum and Huldah, come with me."

The king's garden lay close to the palace. Twenty-five stone steps led up to the wall that separated this garden from the Temple mount. Huldah and Shallum sat together on a bench. Clouds unraveled to let in the winter sunshine, and blue of the heavens reflected in the garden's pool.

Enosh opened a door, and the pharaoh hound darted into the garden. With Josiah running after him, they raced around the paths until the dog panted to a stop in front of Huldah.

Josiah wrinkled his nose. "It's no fun just to sit on a throne all day. I like to play once in awhile." He raised his head. "I hear something." Dashing away, he climbed the steps to the gate in the Temple mount's wall.

Alarmed, Shallum hurried after him. Together they descended, and Josiah called to Enosh, "I heard a boy's voice in the Temple courtyard. Go find out who he is and bring him to me." When he spoke to Huldah, his eyes danced in happy anticipation. "I have only my little brother to play with, but maybe I can have a friend too." He squatted on the path with his arm around the dog.

Enosh entered the garden, pushing a squirming child in front of him. "Here's the boy. His father's a priest, a Benjaminite from Anathoth. He comes once a year to take his turn offering sacrifices in the Temple. This year he brought his son along."

"My name is Jeremiah," shouted the boy.

A Benjaminite from Anathoth. Remembering the night that Shallum tried to kidnap Josiah and take him away, Huldah glanced at her husband.

"I know his father, this priest from Anathoth," he said. "He's a good man."

Jeremiah stopped squirming and glared at the hound. "I've never seen a dog like that before. He doesn't look like one of those mean, wild dogs that run around in packs."

"He's not mean. He's a pharaoh hound," Josiah explained. "When I became king, my mother gave me her dog."

"What's his name?"

"Nebka."

"Is that an Egyptian dog? Egyptians are bad."

"Their dogs are good. Come on, I'll show you." He darted away with the dog at his heels.

For a moment Jeremiah hesitated. Then he ran after the king and his pet.

Enosh laughed. "I think the court session is finished for today. The officials will have to wait."

Huldah glanced up at one of the windows overlooking the garden. She recognized lean, dark-eyed Zophar and another courtier scowling at the boys as they played with Josiah's dog. Although she couldn't hear what the men were saying, the sound of their voices conveyed annoyance. She touched her husband's arm. "The courtiers are not happy with our new king."

Shallum dragged his attention away from the boys and the dog. "Why can't they give him a chance?" he grumbled. "He'll show he's not like his father."

Huldah shook her head. "I'm afraid they want all the power for themselves."

Enosh surveyed the windows. "I'll assign a strong group of soldiers to guard Josiah." Speaking directly to Shallum, he added, "Since you're keeper of his wardrobe, you will spend time with him each day and can watch over him in his private chambers."

And who'll watch over my husband? Huldah wondered.

* * *

Now when Huldah accompanied Shallum outside the city walls to carry water to travelers, she noticed that he proceeded cautiously at the gate and wherever one of Zophar's followers might lurk. Walking to the palace, he slowed his pace at each turn in the streets. One day a large stone fell from the top of a wall, barely missing Shallum's head. When Enosh found out, he ordered extra soldiers to patrol the streets through which Shallum and Huldah passed. And so the months went by and then the years without further mishaps.

As for Josiah, with soldiers to protect him even as he walked through the palace halls, the boy king avoided calamity and retained the throne.

Each spring the almond trees in the king's garden unfolded their scented blossoms. One spring day Josiah sat alone in the garden except for his dog and two guards who stood by the door to a passageway, but he didn't notice the almonds' fragrance. The pharaoh hound sprawled on the bench beside him while Josiah held its slender head in his lap. The dog breathed heavily and with difficulty.

One of the guards opened the door to allow Enosh to enter. Josiah looked up. "I told the guards to let no one near me until after my dog dies."

"Please forgive me," replied Enosh. "Your friend Jeremiah has just arrived from the north. He was so eager to see you, he came in his traveling clothes and has managed to talk his way past all the guards. Right now he's standing at the door to this garden."

"If Jeremiah can do that, let him in."

When his friend strode toward him, Josiah managed to give him a faint smile. "I'm glad you came."

Jeremiah knelt by the dog and stroked its back. "What's wrong with Nebka?"

"My doctors say he's old and tired . . . and ready to die."

"I'll wait with you." He situated himself at the other end of the bench. They sat quietly, saying little. In the distance, migrating turtledoves crooned their wistful calls. Nearer, in the stables, horses stomped. The pharaoh hound breathed softly one last time. Josiah smoothed the fur on its head.

Jeremiah placed his hand on the dog's back. "We'll miss him. My father says that when death strikes, we must turn to the Lord for comfort."

"That's what Huldah says too."

After the servants wrapped the hound's body in linen strips and buried it under one of the garden's almond trees, Jeremiah again sat with his friend. Josiah was the first to speak. "The high priest Hilkiah has been advising me to take a wife."

"A wife! Do you want to?"

Josiah shrugged his shoulders. "I don't know, but now that I'm almost 16, I guess it's time. Hilkiah says it's good to strengthen our ties with the outlying districts. He suggested a girl named Hamutal of Libnah."

"Have you ever seen her? Is she pretty?"

"I haven't seen her. Hilkiah says that's not important. What we need, besides gaining support from all of Judah, is to continue following the wishes of the courtiers and the citizens of Jerusalem." Josiah paused to think deeply before he added, "I need to ask Huldah's advice."

"Huh!" Jeremiah snorted. "How come you're always asking Huldah's advice?"

Josiah stood up. "I ask her advice because I trust her. Don't listen to what the courtiers and some of the priests say. They don't like Huldah because she's been telling me to get rid of the altars to Baal and other foreign idols." His voice grew calmer. "As soon as I can, I'm going to start reforms in this kingdom."

Jeremiah's voice revealed his excitement. "My father says you should get rid of all the altars and also the high places, where priests sacrifice to foreign idols. When are you going to start doing it?"

Josiah frowned in deep concentration. "The Assyrians aren't as strong as they were when they took my grandfather away, but we still have to watch out for the Babylonians and the Egyptians."

Jeremiah jumped to his feet. "Fight them. Fight them."

"First, I guess I'd better marry that girl from Libnah."

* * *

A few days later Huldah came home early from teaching the ladies in the palace. Although the afternoon was warm and sunshine still touched the courtyard wall, she hugged her cloak more tightly to her body. Preoccupied with the news she had heard, she was only dimly aware of the aroma of bread baking and the rattling of pots and dishes as the cooks prepared the evening meal.

At last the welcome sound of Shallum's footsteps echoed in the street. When he entered the courtyard, she ran to him. "I must talk to you."

He put his arm around her shoulders. "Is what you have to talk about so important that it can't wait until after the evening meal?"

Chapter 11

Miriama told me that Josiah is going to be married, " Huldah blurted, "and Hilkiah has advised him to take not only one wife but two."

"Come and sit down." Shallum led her to a couch in his room. "That's not unusual. Most kings marry more than one woman."

She leaned against him. "Yes, I know that's true, but Josiah is so young. It's hard enough to lose him to this girl Hamutal but the other one is Zebidah. She's two years older than Josiah."

"He's no longer a little boy," her husband gently reminded her, "and we have to remember that he's not our son. These brides come from outer territories, and Hilkiah realizes we must strengthen Jerusalem's ties with these districts. We need them to help resist attack from Babylon or Egypt." He tightened his embrace. "But foreign powers are not the only threats to Josiah."

Huldah stiffened and raised her head from his shoulder. "What do you mean?"

"Josiah talks of making reforms, of destroying all the foreign idols and their altars." Shallum stood up and faced his wife. "But Zophar and his followers are stirring up opposition. He's telling the citizens this could bring on an invasion."

Huldah held her hands over her eyes. "Since Josiah was a little boy, I've told him that the Temple needs repair and that the people of Judah should stop worshiping idols. I didn't think his own courtiers would turn against him. What can such a young king do?"

"He can at least marry those girls from the territories of Libnah and Rumah."

She took a deep breath and sighed, "If this is the only way to strengthen the kingdom, I suppose I must accept it."

* * *

During the following month, the people of Jerusalem prepared for the marriage of King Josiah to Hamutal. The rhythmic notes of flutes and the percussion of cymbals filled the air while musicians practiced their songs. Women and girls went out to the hills and gathered palm branches, yellow daisies, and a variety of lilies to decorate the city. The morning of the wedding, wealthy citizens donned their finest robes and draped golden chains around their necks. Even beggars washed their faces and hands for the festive occasion.

In the women's quarters of the palace, Hamutal's mother and the court ladies adorned the bride in a silk gown, golden in color and festooned with rows of emeralds and pearls.

Huldah sat in the queen's reception room with Jedidah and Miriama.

"Soon everyone will know me as queen *mother*," Jedidah said softly.

Miriama shook her head. "You will always remain our queen." Huldah nodded in agreement.

The piping of flutes and beat of cymbals indicated that Josiah was coming for his bride. Jedidah, Huldah, and Miriama followed Hamutal and her attendants into the women's garden, where the groom waited. A lump caught in Huldah's throat as she watched the bride's father remove the veil that covered Hamutal's face and place it on Josiah's shoulder.

Flanked by a strong guard of armed soldiers and attended by men and women of the court, the king and his bride went out to parade through Jerusalem's streets. Then they returned to the palace, where music and feasting continued far into the night.

A month later Josiah ordered all these festivities repeated for his marriage to Zebidah. Along with Jedidah and Miriama, Huldah again listened to the flutes and cymbals. She watched the bride, who was dressed in a blue silk gown decorated with discs of gold, step regally forward to her groom.

Josiah's mother wiped tears from her eyes. Huldah and Miriama put their arms around her and led her back to her chambers.

* * *

Nearly a year passed before Jeremiah returned to Jerusalem. Immediately he sought out the young king. Guards allowed him to enter the royal court and wait in the smallest reception room.

As soon as Josiah came in, Jeremiah confronted him. "I thought you said you were going to make some reforms.

93

When are you going to begin?"

Josiah closed the door to the passageway, shutting out the guards who waited there. "I want to be a good king like my ancestor David, but I have to proceed slowly. Some of the courtiers are against any reforms, and if I act too quickly, they might try to seize control."

"Looks to me like all you've done so far is provide a couple of heirs to the throne."

"Now that I have a son with each of my wives, my enemies are more eager than ever to rid themselves of the royal family."

"Enosh and his guards are loyal to you, and the high priest wants to throw out the idols," Jeremiah snorted. "What are you waiting for?"

Josiah raised his voice. "For the right time."

"When?" shouted Jeremiah.

Josiah tapped his friend on the shoulder. "You're beginning to shout like a prophet."

"Not me. Just because I'm loud doesn't mean I'm going to become a prophet. I wouldn't want to be one."

"You sure sound like one."

Jeremiah walked to a window and gazed out to the southern hills. "Huldah's a prophet, but she doesn't shout."

Josiah joined him at the window. "God uses people in different ways. Huldah works in her own quiet way. Right now she's helping me study the scrolls we have so I can find out what the Lord wants me to do. You could go out in the streets and shout. What are you waiting for?"

"Like you, for the right time." Jeremiah pressed his lips together.

* * *

Up in the palace Huldah finished the reading lesson for

the day. As the ladies filed out the doorway, she placed the library scrolls on a shelf in her schoolroom. A few minutes later she joined Jedidah in the queen mother's chambers. A maidservant brought dates and almonds and offered them to Huldah. While she munched the fruit and nuts, her attention focused on Jedidah.

The queen mother twisted her hands together and stared at the floor. Finally she looked up. "I'm concerned about Josiah."

Huldah made an effort to keep her reply calm. "In what way?"

"I'm proud of my son. Even though he's young, he makes wise decisions, but now he's determined to begin those reforms, to cleanse the Temple of foreign idols and their altars." Jedidah shook her head. "Isn't that what I've wanted? Isn't that what you and I have hoped he would do? Now that he says he will, why am I terrified?"

Before Huldah could answer, a maidservant announced that the king had arrived to visit his mother. The women stood up to greet the young man. *How handsome he is!* Huldah mused. *Tall and slender like his father, but he has the thick dark hair and slightly darker skin from his mother's clan.* The start of a beard showed on his face.

He strode in and kissed Jedidah on both cheeks and then kissed Huldah. Seating himself on a couch, he announced, "I've come to inform you of my plans." At his words, sudden fear stabbed Huldah. She looked toward the door, wishing to escape even the knowledge of what he proposed to undertake.

On the opposite couch, Jedidah drew in a shaky breath. "We're listening. Please tell us."

"We can't go on forever allowing some priests to offer sacrifices to foreign idols. And the Temple itself is in terrible condition. Gold falls from the ceiling and disappears. For years cracks have appeared in the walls and the floor. New materials are needed." Josiah stood up and pounded his right fist into his other hand. "I'm going to order repairs."

"How will you pay for these repairs?" his mother asked.

"Taxes. I'll have to tax the people of Judah."

"They won't like more taxes."

"I know," replied her son thoughtfully. "That's why I must proceed slowly—just a little increase at a time. We'll save the silver and gold that's collected until we have enough to start repairing the Temple and removing the idols."

Huldah swallowed hard. "You must take great care. Zophar and his followers will never agree to these reforms."

Josiah sighed. "You're right. But I would rather follow what God wants me to do than what some men want." He smiled at Jedidah and Huldah. "Isn't that what you have taught me for as long as I can remember?"

The women looked at each other but said nothing.

"When we have collected enough silver to pay their wages," Josiah continued, "we can hire carpenters, builders, and masons. We'll need to buy timber and quarry stone. Gold we'll use to beautify the Temple. All this may take a few years, but I assure you we shall have reform in Judah while I am king. I will no longer serve the interests of foreign powers nor my own subjects who wish to serve them."

He rose from the couch and stepped close to his mother. Taking her hands in his, he spoke softly, "Don't worry. God is with us." He smiled reassuringly at Huldah and left the room.

The women sat in stunned silence until Huldah said, "Josiah's plans are right and good."

"Yes, but at what price?" Jedidah sobbed. "With what danger to Josiah?"

* * *

During the summer the young king sent town criers into the streets of Jerusalem to announce that he was increasing taxes. Messengers rode out to all parts of Judah to inform the people that Josiah needed money to repair the Temple.

"Why should we send our silver and gold to Jerusalem?" some grumbled. "We can worship at the high places in our own territory."

Others disagreed. "Finally we have a good king who is ruling like his ancestor David. We will do as he asks."

* * *

At her booth in the marketplace one afternoon, Huldah prepared to return home. Many citizens had sought her counsel that day, asking that she inquire of the Lord about paying extra taxes to repair the Temple. As she stepped out of the booth, a familiar figure walked toward her. Even after all these years of marriage, her heart still gave a leap of excitement when she saw Shallum in the marketplace.

"Will you walk with me to the Mount of Olives on this lovely summer afternoon?"

She touched his hand. "I will."

Outside the walls, they strolled into the Kidron Valley and wandered part way up the mount. An old shepherd woman sat quietly watching a few sheep. Near her, two small boys played with stones and sticks.

Farther along the hillside Huldah and Shallum found a

comfortable resting place under the gray-green leaves of a young olive tree.

Sitting close together in comfortable silence, they gazed across the valley. A soft breeze brought the pungent scent of thyme blossoms. As she admired Solomon's Temple and the beloved city of Jerusalem, words from one of her scrolls came to mind. "How lovely is thy dwelling place, O Lord of hosts."

Becoming aware of the little boys calling to each other, Huldah said, "I'm sorry."

Puzzled, Shallum looked at her. "Why are you sorry on a beautiful day like this?"

"Because I've given you no sons, not even a daughter. You'll never have grandsons."

He laid his hand against her cheek to turn her face toward his. "We have Josiah—at least in our hearts we have him."

"Josiah," she echoed but could say no more. And then she heard a whimper, a faint sound from somewhere on the hill behind them. Something was crying. She twisted around to find the source of the noise. From a bush a small brown puppy tumbled down the hillside and landed in Huldah's lap. It looked up at her with big brown eyes. Wiggling to its feet it jumped up to lick her face.

Shallum chuckled. "This little animal likes you."

Trying to calm the excited puppy, Huldah held it in her arms and stroked its back. "It probably belongs to those boys. I'll take it to them."

When the shepherd woman saw Huldah with the dog, she looked the other way.

"Is this your puppy?" Huldah asked.

"No, it's a stray. I don't want it. I have enough to care for with my sheep and my grandsons."

The little dog's eyes pleaded with Huldah. "You're so thin," she said.

Shallum patted its head. "Shall we take him home with us?"

She wrapped the end of her shawl around the puppy and hugged it to her. "Since keeping dogs is an Egyptian custom, they're not welcome in the city." She shook her head. "But if we leave this one here, he'll starve."

"I know a couple of city officials who have dogs."

The puppy squirmed and Huldah tightened her hold. "Let's keep him."

All the way to the city and through the streets, she cuddled the warm puppy under her shawl and planned where she might make a bed for it in her room.

But when they stopped at their courtyard gate, her attention shifted from the little dog to the anxious face of the doorkeeper. Before they could enter the courtyard, he informed Shallum, "A messenger arrived to say that you are wanted in the king's royal court immediately."

Chapter 12

"At this time of day!" exclaimed Huldah.

"If Josiah needs me, I must go," her husband replied.

"Yes of course," she agreed, but as soon as he went out the gate, she wanted to call him back. Perhaps Josiah had not sent the message.

At the royal court Shallum followed the sounds of angry voices to the large reception room, where Josiah sat rigidly on the ivory throne.

Zophar's loud words carried above the noisy gathering. "If we remove idols and their altars from the Temple, we can expect to receive the wrath of foreign powers."

"If we do not remove them," replied Josiah, "we can expect to receive the wrath of God."

The authoritative voice of the high priest Hilkiah quieted the assembly. "The time has come to cleanse the Temple."

In support of the king and the priest, Shallum spoke. "When enough money has come in for needed repairs to the Temple, many men will have work. With wages to stonemasons, carpenters, and other artisans, we can expect a time of prosperity."

Zophar's fierce eyes glared at Shallum. "What about the royal court? If the Temple can have gold on the ceiling, why can't the court have it too?" He turned to Josiah. "Prosperity will come just as easily if you divert tax money for courtiers to use."

Josiah stood up and pulled himself as tall as possible. "I will follow the counsel of my advisor Hilkiah. The time has come to remove the idols and repair the Temple. I, your king, have spoken." He raised his hand. "All of you except Hilkiah have my permission to leave. The high priest and I will formulate plans."

Zophar shot a glance, angry and threatening, at Shallum. Deliberately ignoring Zophar's hostility, Shallum turned away. Then with all the courtiers and priests except Hilkiah, he backed out of the room.

The king sat down on the throne with the high priest standing next to him.

Seven days later riders left Jerusalem for all parts of Judah, advising the people about an additional increase in taxes to repair the Temple. Over the next months silver and gold accumulated slowly. Temple doorkeepers collected the tax money, and Hilkiah placed it in a large storage chest. He ordered his most trusted guards to watch over it in an underground chamber.

As spring changed to summer and then to autumn, citizens came to Huldah and demanded, "When will Josiah start hiring workers for repair of the Temple?"

"I only interpret messages from the Lord," she told each one. "I don't know when our king will begin his reforms."

While the people grumbled, other springs passed.

Returning home one afternoon, Huldah watched the dog bound across the stones to welcome her. She and Shallum had named him Yaphe and with infinite patience had trained him to obey. Now the large, brown mongrel sat down and waited for her to rub behind his long ears and over his backbone.

Huldah knelt to pat him. When she walked to her room, he followed her and lay down near her hearth. She removed her cloak and put away the papyrus that she had carried with her. Hearing her husband at the gate, she instructed Yaphe, "Go to Shallum."

He raced out of the room and across the courtyard. Smiling, Huldah stood in the doorway to observe the dog's exuberant greeting of his master.

After giving Yaphe a pat, Shallum hurried across the courtyard to his wife.

Observing his quick stride, her smile faded and misgiving seized her. "Has something happened to Josiah?"

"Just the opposite. Today he ordered the priests to remove one of Baal's altars from the Temple. Nubian slaves have hammered it into pieces so they can carry the heavy stone." He started toward the gate. "Come with me and we'll go out to watch them dump the pieces."

Huldah followed him to the gate. "At last! At last the time is here."

In the street other citizens were headed toward the northern gate. "The word has spread," said Shallum.

"Wait!" Huldah stopped walking. "Why is everyone going this way? Shouldn't we be going to the Hinnom? That's where King Manasseh threw the altars and idols when he cleansed the Temple."

"No. Josiah ordered his slaves to carry the altar to the northern part of the Kidron where the valley is wider and not as steep."

"I've always considered the Hinnom the valley of evil and the Kidron the valley of good."

"Don't worry," advised her husband. "After the slaves have hammered this altar to dust, the Kidron will remain as good as ever."

"Perhaps some day," mused Huldah, "it will even have a brook running through it."

Outside the wall and following a wide path, they arrived at a place where it sloped downward. "There they are," exclaimed Shallum, "and they've already started to beat the pieces into dust." Slaves and soldiers worked side by side, pounding at the stones.

Huldah grabbed her husband's arm. "There's Josiah!"

"He's watching to make sure that nothing but dust will remain of that altar."

She sighed contentedly. "A good king, always doing what is right in the eyes of the Lord."

A woman standing near her spoke up. "But not in the sight of the enemies of Judah."

Shallum placed his hand on top of Huldah's, giving warmth and reassurance.

The sound of pounding continued. Dust drifted, bringing with it the smell of ashes from the many sacrifices the priests of Baal had burned on the stone. The sun set and the blue of the western sky turned soft orange. Torches appeared in the Kidron and work continued. "They will stay until nothing remains," said Shallum. "We can go home, knowing that Josiah will make sure it happens."

From that day, workmen, soldiers, and priests continued to remove the altars of the Baals, their incense stands, and the poles and images of Asherah.

"Beat them into dust," the king ordered, "and strew that dust over the tombs of those who have sacrificed to these idols."

That spring and summer, Josiah, along with Enosh and a contingent of soldiers, rode to the outer territories of Judah. They directed their horses from one high place to another to oversee the destruction of pagan worship.

In Jerusalem's marketplace, Huldah looked up from the scroll she was reading to see Jeremiah standing at the door to her booth. Although three years younger than Josiah and not as tall, he had grown into a sturdy young man.

"I've left Anathoth, and now I live at Solomon's Temple," he announced.

"Will you come in and tell me more?"

He sat on a bench across the table from her and frowned at the wall. "The Lord is calling me to become a prophet, but how can I? I'm too young, and I'd rather be a priest like my father. I didn't mind shouting at Josiah about how slow he was to start cleansing the country of idols. He's my friend. But where can I find words to shout at other people?"

Remembering Shallum's advice to her many years before, Huldah repeated it for this troubled young man. "If the Lord has chosen you to prophesy, you must accept."

"Why does He need me? I can't speak well enough. He already has the prophets Zephaniah and Nahum in Judah, and they both speak better than I can."

"He will put words into your mouth."

Jeremiah sat silently looking at the floor before he spoke doubtfully. "If I did prophesy, where would He want me to begin?"

Huldah glanced at the steady stream of shoppers passing in the street. "Right here in the marketplace. Even when all the images and altars are gone, in their hearts some Judeans will still worship false gods." She reached across the table and touched his arm. "The Lord has called you to admonish the people and warn them of destruction if they continue in their evil ways."

After hesitating for a moment Jeremiah determined, "I'll do it." He pushed into the crowd of shoppers, and his voice rang out. "Thus says the Lord. 'My people have changed their glory for useless things. My people have done two evils. They have forsaken Me, the source of living waters, and they have dug cisterns for themselves—broken cisterns that hold no water.' "

Huldah saw people staring at Jeremiah, and some backed away from him. She closed her eyes and raised her head. "Thank You, Lord, for this young prophet." Opening her eyes she saw a man standing at her door.

"Who's that out here shouting at us?" he demanded to know.

Huldah stood up to face him. "He is Judah's newest prophet."

The man shook his head and walked away.

* * *

During the next six years, King Josiah continued his search throughout the land for evidences of pagan worship. At the same time, he directed workmen to proceed with repairs in the Temple. Yet in the outlying districts, the people still burned incense to foreign gods, and secretly some of Jerusalem's citizens worshiped idols.

One summer morning Huldah relaxed in her courtyard before walking to the marketplace. Embroidering on a new woolen shawl, she thrust a bone needle through the white woven fabric, stitching a floral design with red, yellow, and green yarn.

Near her feet Yaphe lolled comfortably on the warm courtyard stones. At the sound of hurrying footsteps in the street, he raised his head and growled. A voice at the gate rang out, "Open for the high priest Hilkiah."

The dog barked. Huldah leaned toward him. "Quiet," she said while motioning for a maid to take the dog into the servants' quarters. She laid her embroidery on the bench and stood up to welcome this distinguished visitor to her home. But why hadn't he talked to Shallum at the palace? Her heart pounded in fear. Had something so drastic happened that even the high priest would come to inform her? She adjusted her lightweight yellow robe and smoothed her hair with both hands.

The doorkeeper swung open the heavy gate. "Welcome to the house of Shallum, keeper of the king's wardrobe, and Huldah, the prophetess."

Hilkiah marched in, and four men followed him. Huldah recognized the scribe Shaphan and his son with two other officials from Josiah's court. The priest greeted her. "Peace."

She bowed to him. "Peace. I'm sorry my husband is not at home to receive your call, but please enter his reception chamber. I'll instruct the cooks to prepare refreshments for you to partake while a servant runs to the palace to inform my husband that you are waiting for him." She motioned for a manservant to show the guests into the receiving room.

"Wait! Don't waste our time with refreshments." Hilkiah's demand checked her from entering the kitchen. "We will sit in Shallum's reception chamber, but we have not come here to speak with him. We are here to talk to you." The men strode across the courtyard and into the room that the servant indicated.

To me? Huldah wondered. *These important men have come all the way to my home to talk to me?* She followed them into the room.

Hilkiah sat formally on a carved oak chair. His elaborate robe, woven with golden threads through it, draped over his ample frame. In his hands he held a scroll yellowed with age. The four officials stood behind him.

He cleared his throat. "As you know, those of us who are Levites have been collecting and guarding silver and gold for restoring the Temple. Yesterday after we paid wages to carpenters and builders and masons, I found a large scroll in the bottom of the storage chest." He shifted uneasily on his chair. "I don't know who hid it in that place."

Huldah took a step forward, eager to read what the scroll contained, but instead of handing it to her, the high priest continued to explain. "I showed it to the scribe Shaphan, who read it to the king." Hilkiah shook his head and ordered, "Shaphan, tell Josiah's reaction."

The scribe stood up. "When he heard the words, our king tore his clothes and moaned that the wrath of God is kindled against us. Then he appointed the five of us to carry the scroll to you for further interpretation."

Hilkiah held out the large roll of papyrus toward her. "Read it now so that we can return to King Josiah with your prophecy."

With eager hands she reached for the scroll. Brittle with age, it felt light and vulnerable. She placed it on a side table and unrolled the first section. For a moment Huldah was sensitive to the men watching her, but when she began to read, nothing entered her mind except the Lord's words that an ancient scribe had recorded.

His writing warns of consequences whenever people depart from worship of the Lord, Huldah reflected silently. *This law book curses the disobedient with doom. How true it is that our people are as disloyal to God today as at any time in our history!*

After reading the entire scroll, she remained in deep thought with her chin cupped in her hand. The words she had read were not just history. They were holy words. God's true revelation. Her eyes widened in sudden insight. For many years she had read scrolls without realizing that the words were truly sacred. Only today, from this book of law, the Lord revealed to her that she was reading Holy Scripture.

Hilkiah's voice reached into her consciousness. "What do you understand from these writings?"

Slowly she stood up and faced him. "You have brought Holy Scripture for me to interpret. Tell King Josiah that the Lord says, 'Because they have forsaken Me and have burned incense unto others gods, I will bring evil upon this place and upon the inhabitants thereof. My wrath shall be kindled against this place, and shall not be quenched.' "

The priest turned pale. He grabbed the neck of his robe as if to tear it. Instead he lowered his hands to the arm of the chair and heaved himself to his feet.

"Please wait," begged Huldah. "There is more to the message." She bowed her head, unable to continue.

"Hurry and tell me so I can report to the king," insisted Hilkiah.

With great effort she composed herself enough to speak. "It's too late for the people of Judah, yet for our king the Lord says, 'Because you have humbled yourself and torn your clothes and wept before Me, I have heard you. Therefore I will gather you to your grave in peace. Your eyes shall not see all the evil which I will bring upon this place.' "

For a moment Hilkiah stared at Huldah. Then he picked up the scroll. "So be it. I will inform King Josiah." Solemnly he walked out the door and across the courtyard. The other men followed.

Huldah dropped to her knees and bent her head to the floor. "Lord," she groaned, "why have the inhabitants of

Judah brought this disaster upon the land so that Josiah must die while still young?" Finding no answer to her question, she stood up and told herself, "Now I must go to my booth in the marketplace."

When she walked across the courtyard to the gate, the dog ran out of the servants' quarters. Looking up with eager brown eyes, he asked to go with her.

"No," she cautioned, "you can't go with me. Wait here for Shallum. When he comes, he'll take you for a run along the Kidron Valley."

Sadly the dog lay down to wait.

In the city center, the shopkeepers called out their wares. "Pomegranates, pomegranates. Nice and ripe. Ready to eat." "Fresh dates. Just arrived from the south."

The familiar scene and the people in it appeared peaceful, harmless. Yet after reading the scroll from the Temple, Huldah sensed anew the evil in their hearts. Even Jeremiah's loud warnings went unheeded.

She entered her booth in the marketplace, and while waiting for citizens to come for advice, she sat down to read the words of Isaiah from a papyrus she carried with her. "For you have forgotten the God of your salvation, and have not remembered the Rock of your refuge." The prophet Isaiah had given this warning more than 100 years before. Now she and Jeremiah must repeat it. Some time after midday the shouting of town criers echoed throughout the marketplace. "King Josiah has declared that tomorrow before the sun is high, all citizens must assemble on the Temple mount. Each and every one must come."

Men crowded into Huldah's booth. "Why has the king summoned us to the Temple mount?" "What does this mean?"

"King Josiah will inform us tomorrow," was all she would tell them.

The following morning Huldah and Shallum walked together through the city streets. She glanced at him. "How many years have passed since we took Josiah here?"

"Twenty-six years ago we brought him to the priest for redemption. How much our life has revolved around him all this time!"

"And now we're with him again on the Temple mount." Her voice shook. "But this time he's here to tell the people about their unredeemed sin."

Shallum held her hand while they climbed the path to the mount. After passing through the gate, they saw that a crowd had already gathered.

"I'll have to leave you here," explained Shallum. "Josiah plans to stand by a pillar on the Temple porch and has asked me and some of his most trusted officials to stay near him." He threaded his way through the rapidly growing crowd.

Near Huldah the limestone Temple rose high. As she walked slowly forward, the voices of the people around her faded away. She was aware only of this sacred place. Although she had never seen the inside of the building, she knew there was beauty in the Holy of Holies, where two cherubim guarded the precious Ark of the Covenant.

Someone bumped into her, and she felt rough hands on her arm. "Stop," a voice hissed. "Go no farther."

Chapter 13

Zophar! Take your hands off my arm."

"Not until you hear what I have to say." Huldah tried to pull away but his grip proved too strong. He pushed his face close to hers. "The king should have taken that scroll to a prophet, not a woman who claims to be one. Now he plans to honor you by telling your interpretation to all of Jerusalem. I'm warning you. Stop this prophesying, and tell Shallum to give up his position in the court. If you don't do as I say, dire consequences lie ahead for you, your husband, and the king." With a last threatening glance at her, he forced his way through the crowd until she could no longer see him.

Shaken from the encounter, Huldah edged forward until the crowd blocked her way. When she raised herself onto her toes, she could see Josiah dressed in a purple robe richly decorated with golden embroidery. Shallum, wearing a robe of brown and white stripes, stood behind him on the Temple porch. She caught a glimpse of Jeremiah on the other side. Miriama and Queen Mother

Jedidah waited at the front of the crowd with Josiah's wives and children. Searching through the multitude, Huldah finally spotted her father, mother, and Kezia standing together.

How soon could she talk to her husband? Huldah ached to know. How soon could she warn him about Zophar's threat?

The king's voice rang out for the people to hear. "Our high priest, Hilkiah, has found a scroll that someone stored in the Temple many years ago." While Josiah read the scroll to them, the citizens listened with growing agitation. The sun climbed higher into the sky, and still the words of destruction pounded at them. ". . .You shall serve your enemies whom the Lord will send against you. . . . And the Lord will scatter you among all peoples, from one end of the earth to the other. . . . And there shall be no rest for the sole of your foot. . . ."

Handing the scroll to a waiting courtier, the king announced, "Yesterday I ordered Hilkiah to take the book to the prophetess Huldah for interpretation. She has informed me that this writing is Holy Scripture." When he disclosed her prediction that God would bring evil upon them, the people broke into great wailing and lamentation.

Josiah lifted his hand for silence. "Today I am making a covenant before the Lord. I will keep His commandments and His testimonies and His statutes. With all my heart and with all my soul, I will perform the words of the covenant that are written in this book. From this day forward I will remove the abominations out of the land. All the people will serve the Lord their God, and Him only will they serve."

After pausing briefly, Josiah added, "During the past six years, we have already begun reforms, but because of continued disobedience to our Lord, fearful curses will fall upon us. Still if we return to the laws God gave us in this book, there is hope for our descendants and promise that our land will endure forever."

He gazed across the great gathering of his subjects. Then Enosh and his guards opened a passageway through the assembly to escort the king, the royal family, and all courtiers back to the palace. Walking tall and proud, Josiah nodded to the citizens. Shallum followed closely behind him.

A man standing near Huldah addressed another citizen. "I hope this great evil doesn't come during my lifetime."

"If King Josiah casts out every idol," the other replied, "maybe the evil won't come upon us at all."

A third man joined the conversation. "I'm going to follow the example of our king and worship only the Lord, the God of our fathers."

Murmuring in apprehension, the people began to leave the Temple area. Desperately trying to reach Shallum, Huldah pushed her way through the crowd. As men and women bumped into her, she realized that she could not possibly overtake her husband before he descended the steps into the king's garden.

There was only one way to find him. Ask Miriama for help. She turned and, shaking with impatience, continued with the crowd across the mount to the outer wall and then down the path that led through the small valley separating the hill from the city.

Sighing at their slow pace, she listened to women expressing their fear and men discussing the contents of the scroll. Only when they passed into the city streets was she able to quicken her steps. At last with the causeway to the palace ahead of her, Huldah broke into a run. At the outer gate the guards challenged her.

"Huldah, the prophetess and wife of Shallum, keeper of the king's wardrobe," she identified herself, fretting at the formality when the guards already knew her.

After again telling her name to the guards outside the women's garden, they admitted her. She ran along the path and asked the Nubians to open the door to the women's quarters. Inside she climbed the stairway to Jedidah's chambers and called, "Miriama, open for Huldah. Please hurry."

A maidservant swung open the door, and Huldah stumbled in. "Where's Miriama?"

Jedidah appeared at the door to her inner rooms. "Huldah! What is it?"

She took a deep breath and her words tumbled out. "Zophar has threatened Josiah and Shallum and me."

Jedidah came across the room and grabbed Huldah's hands. "We must warn Josiah and Shallum."

"Where's Miriama?" Huldah cried. "She could relay the message."

"She went home with her children." Jedidah's voice shook. "But it's no use to send a message. Josiah and Shallum aren't in the palace or the royal court."

"Not here!"

"No. To answer any questions the citizens might have, Josiah decided to tour the city. Shallum and Enosh and others went with him. They just now left the royal court."

Huldah let go of Jedidah's hands. "Then I will go."

"Where?"

"Into the city to look for them."

"You'll need help." Jedidah glanced at the maid standing near the windows. "I'll send some of my servants with you."

Huldah stepped away from her friend. "No! They

114

would just slow me down." She pulled open the door and hurried away.

* * *

In Jerusalem most of the women had returned to their homes, but men roamed through the streets, talking with their neighbors, questioning anyone they met about the message their king had read to them. Vendors set up a lively business as the men bought food and drink to quench their anxiety.

"Where's King Josiah now?" Huldah asked a shopkeeper.

He pointed down the street. "I'm told he's near the scribes' quarters."

Making her way along the narrow streets, she turned a corner and came upon a familiar figure standing outside the scribes' quarters. "Father!"

Barak frowned at her. "Daughter, what are you doing alone in the streets? The way these citizens are drinking, riots could result. Some are even resenting your interpretation of the writings in the scroll. Why haven't you gone home?"

Quickly she related what Zophar had said.

Her father took hold of her arm. "I'm escorting you to your house where you'll be safe. That's where you belong."

"But Shallum and Josiah. Someone has to tell them."

"Soldiers are with them. No one is going to attack Shallum or Josiah today."

Suddenly all her energy drained away, and Huldah allowed Barak to take her home. After he left, she wandered around her courtyard, unable to concentrate on anything except the thought, *When will Shallum come? Will I be able to warn him soon enough?* Finally with the dog Yaphe at her feet, she sat on a bench and quietly listened for her husband's footsteps. But the only sounds were a sparrow chirping to defend its territory and the cooks in the kitchen starting to prepare the evening meal.

The blue of the clear sky grew darker. The two men who served as night guards arrived to take up their post outside the gate. Huldah heard them conversing in low tones. The first star showed faint light, and still Shallum didn't come. A maidservant lit the courtyard torches. Shallum's menservants returned from the streets.

"Have you seen the master of this household," Huldah asked them. They shrugged their shoulders and shook their heads. As she forced herself to her room for a heavier shawl to ward off the cool night air, the gatekeeper announced, "Master Shallum is coming."

With Yaphe prancing beside her, Huldah ran across the courtyard to her husband. "I've been worried."

He held her in his arms and stroked her back. "The people asked many questions, and Josiah refused to leave until he had answered every one. But why were your worried? You knew I was with Josiah."

"On the Temple mount Zophar talked to me."

"What did he say?"

Huldah pressed her face against his shoulder and sobbed, "He threatened dire consequences for Josiah and for us if you and I don't give up our positions."

"That scoundrel," Shallum growled. "He has no right to threaten us."

The gate guards sounded an alarm. "Men are entering our street."

"Zophar," Huldah gasped.

She heard the challenge of the guards, "What are your intentions?" And then there were groans, then smashing

116

blows sounded against the heavy sycamore door that served as the gate.

"Hide in the storeroom." Shallum pressed her toward it. "And take Yaphe with you." Dashing to his room, he grabbed swords for himself and his menservants, but before he could mobilize for resistance, 10 attackers had broken in and were upon him and his servants.

At the storeroom door, Huldah turned around. The dog barked vigorously and sprang toward the struggling men. Instinctively Huldah ran to her husband and pulled on the arm of the man beating him. He shoved her until she sprawled onto the hard courtyard stones. Yaphe grabbed the attacker's arm in his strong teeth. Cursing, the man kicked the dog, sending him reeling onto the stones.

By the time Huldah was able to lift her head, the men had already dragged Shallum out the gate and down the street. She looked around for help. The two menservants and the doorkeeper lay nearby. "Go after them," she screamed. One of them groaned. She crawled to him and discovered blood covering his face.

Rising to her feet, she looked outside the gate. Yaphe was nowhere to be seen. The guards lay stretched across the doorway. "Zophar and his men," one of them said weakly. "There were too many of them for us."

Huldah stumbled to the kitchen and found the cooks huddled in a corner. "Get the maids to help you bind up the men's wounds," she told them. Returning to the courtyard she called, "Yaphe!" He ran in from the street. "Go to Shallum," she ordered. The dog sniffed at the stones and darted through the open gate.

"Wait!" she called. "Wait for me."

Dutifully, as Shallum had trained him, he sat down until she caught up with him. Sniffing again, he headed toward the city's northern gate.

Oh, no, Huldah thought. *Yaphe expects me to take him for a run in the Kidron Valley and up the mount.* But then in the moonlight she saw him stop and sniff again at the stones before he bounded away, this time toward the city center. She breathed more easily. He was leading her toward the marketplace, where night watchmen outside the shops could tell her what they saw when Zophar and his men passed that way with Shallum.

But instead of continuing toward the marketplace, the dog circled around it. Suddenly he stopped. In a dark doorway a beggar lay sleeping. When Yaphe gave a sharp bark, the man reared up and held his hands in front of him. "Call off your dog."

"He won't harm you. But tell me, have you seen a group of men pass this way?"

"Men come and men go. Some return home very late this night."

Realizing she could gain no help from this beggar, she ordered the dog, "Go to Shallum." On they went through the dark streets. If only she could find a patrol of the king's soldiers, she could try to convince them that she needed help.

A stray cat scurried out of the way, and momentarily Yaphe darted after it. A rat sat atop a homeowner's wall and stared down at Huldah and her dog. Leaning against the wall, two men held flasks of strong drink. She could smell where they had spilled some on their robes. "Aha! A woman. Come join us pretty lady." One held out his flask to her.

Yaphe growled and Huldah asked, "Have you seen men pass this way?"

"Men? Ha. We've seen men pass this way and that way and every way. Now we've even seen a woman and a dog pass this way."

"Go home before you fall down," she muttered in exasperation.

Soon afterward as she turned a corner in the street, Yaphe lay down at her feet and released a low growl. Ahead of them the city wall formed a high barrier. A tall, stone tower rose in threatening reinforcement, and the gate was securely barred.

She held her hands against her chest to control her labored breathing. If Zophar had taken Shallum outside the wall, how could she and the dog leave? Even though they might let men go outside the city at night, would the guards allow a woman to leave?

She stooped to rub Yaphe's back, gaining comfort from his presence.

From the shadow of the tower a harsh voice rang out. "Who are you, and why are you at Valley Gate this time of night?"

Chapter 14

Lord, *keep my voice from trembling,* Huldah prayed silently. She stood up and drew in a deep breath. "I am Huldah, the prophetess, wife of Shallum, keeper of the king's wardrobe."

Two men emerged from the shadow. "If you're really Huldah, wife of Shallum, explain why you are at Valley Gate instead of in his home this time of night."

Yaphe snarled, and the men drew their swords. Huldah leaned down, putting her hand on the dog's neck to restrain him. "Please help me. Evil men attacked my husband. I believe they have taken him outside the city wall. I beg you to send a message to the king that his servant Shallum is in danger." She stood up. "I also beseech you to show your mercy and let me pass through this gate."

Still watching the dog, the men conferred until one announced, "We've come to a decision." He let out a taunting laugh. "We'll allow you to pass so you can see for yourself what's happening in the Hinnom Valley. Wait where you are until we open the gate." They backed away until they stood at the heavily-armored barrier.

Huldah's heart pounded in fearful suspicion. Were these some of Zophar's men posing as Josiah's soldiers? They unbarred the gate. "Pass."

Glancing anxiously from side to side, she hurried through with Yaphe slinking along at her side. The heavy doors clanked behind them. Moonlight revealed a path that descended the valley's steep side. Huldah hunched her shoulders to keep from trembling. The dreaded Hinnom, where Manasseh had sacrificed his children in the fires of Molech! No one wanted to come here even in the daytime. She had never heard of anyone venturing into the Hinnom at night.

The dog sniffed at the rocky ground and gazed up at his mistress. "Go to Shallum," she commanded. They progressed slowly. Huldah stopped often, watching for any sign of movement. A few scrubby cypress trees grew on the valley floor. Men could hide behind them. Part way down, the path turned and ran along the Hinnom's side. Yaphe halted abruptly. Looking upward he growled deep in his throat. High on the opposite side of the valley a pack of wild dogs were dark silhouettes against the sky.

While she waited for her dog to continue along the path, Huldah surveyed the scene below her. "Oh!" she gasped. A group of silent men were lifting a tightly bound figure onto a pile of stones. In the moonlight, Huldah could distinguish Shallum's striped robe. The man on the stone altar was her husband! She held her fist against her lips to stifle the scream that threatened to escape.

"I must do something to help him," she whispered. "But what?" Even if she were able to roll large stones down the hillside, they might hit Shallum instead of his assailants.

Yaphe, watching the dogs, raised his head and gave a howl, long and passionate. The pack answered with soaring howls that sent a shiver through Huldah's body.

The men's attention shifted from their grim task to the opposite side of the valley, where the dogs milled restlessly on the ridge top.

"Go to Shallum," Huldah ordered.

Continuing to bark loudly, Yaphe bounded forward. Excitement carried to the pack, and they leaped down the hillside to join him in a noisy race.

"Dogs!" shouted Zophar. "Wild dogs." He and his henchmen scattered, all running in the direction of the Kidron Valley. The dogs turned and pursued them, nipping at their heels, biting at their legs.

Huldah scrambled down the hillside to her husband. A container of bright coals lay on the ground—hot coals for lighting the altar fire. Moonlight gleamed off a knife that one of the men had dropped—perhaps the very knife he had intended to use on Shallum. She picked it up and quickly cut the cloth that gagged his mouth.

"Huldah, Huldah," he breathed her name. She sawed at the cords that bound his wrists and then worked on the cords around his ankles. Shallum tried to stand up, but stumbled and fell to the ground.

Huldah raised her head, listening to shouts that came from the direction of the Kidron. Yaphe trotted back from the pursuit. He lay down and licked his master's face. Then the dog stood up and looked toward the opposite side of the valley. When Huldah followed his gaze, she groaned, "Oh, no. All the dogs have given up the chase, and they're returning to the ridge."

Shallum pressed his ear to the ground. "I hear footsteps of men coming this way."

Zophar's men returning! She pulled on her husband's

arm. "Hold onto me, and I'll try to pull you up."

He tried to stand but was unable. "You go, Huldah. Go while there's still time."

"No. I'll not leave you here to die at the hands of Zophar." She peered into the shadows, searching for the men whom Shallum heard approaching. A cloud had drifted across the moon, making it difficult for her to see. Was someone moving behind those small cypress trees, or was it only her imagination? If Zophar was returning, how many men were with him?

The pounding of running feet echoed into her ears, and then Zophar's voice sliced through the night air. "I decided not to wait until this woman stopped prophesying. The time has come for both of you to die." In the moonlight, she could see the sword raised high above his head. Behind him, his henchmen drew their weapons.

Struggling to stand, Shallum was able to rise only to his knees.

Huldah stepped forward to face Zophar. "That will not happen."

"Is this one of your prophecies?" he sneered.

How can I divert him, confuse him? The words of Isaiah! "The Lord goes forth like a mighty man, like a man of war He stirs up His fury," she screamed at Zophar. "He cries out, He shouts aloud, He shows himself mighty against His foes."

Zophar laughed derisively. Slight movements in the valley behind him and his men caught Huldah's attention. Dark figures were creeping forward among the cypress. Were they some of the king's soldiers or more of this traitor's followers? "Do not forsake us, O Lord," she prayed quietly. "Make haste to help us."

Suddenly Yaphe jumped forward, baring his sharp

teeth, growling wildly. Zophar and his men backed away from the dog.

"Thus says the Lord. They shall be turned back and utterly put to shame, who trust in graven images, who say to molten images, 'You are our gods.'" She glared at the men facing her. "These words that Isaiah recorded are the Lord's Scripture, holy and true."

A trumpet blared. Yelling an ancient war cry, the king's soldiers sped forward. Zophar and his followers raised their swords, but the soldiers knocked their weapons to the ground. In a few minutes, Josiah's men had bound the traitors' hands and tied ropes around their necks.

At the sight of the king among the soldiers, Shallum called out, "Praise God!"

Josiah rushed to the man on the ground and with a mighty heave pulled him to his feet. "I'm thankful we arrived in time."

More soldiers poured from Valley Gate. Enosh was leading them. He scrambled down the hillside to report to the king. "We have arrested the band of Zophar's followers who had overcome your soldiers at Valley Gate, and now your patrols are searching the city for more."

"Good work," said Josiah. "Tonight these traitors will sit in the dungeon. Tomorrow I'll banish them to the southern wilderness."

Zophar let out a loud wail. "Banish!" he protested. "I do not deserve banishment to the wilderness."

Josiah scowled at him. "A large guard of soldiers on horseback will escort you and all your men, on foot and in chains, to the desert. There they will leave you in the territory of the nomadic tribes." He motioned to Enosh. "Take these vipers to the dungeon."

Exhausted, Huldah stepped closer to her husband.

When he put his arm around her, his warmth gave her renewed strength.

Josiah turned toward them, and his voice shook with emotion. "Huldah, you have once again proven your wisdom. When my soldiers saw a group of men still in the streets, they thought nothing of it. But when a lone woman and a dog appeared, they notified the palace."

"But I found none of your soldiers in the streets," Huldah protested. "How did they see me and my dog?"

"You thought you talked to a beggar and two drunken citizens, but they were really some of my spies. Others that you didn't see waited nearby." Josiah faced Shallum. "You have a brave wife, and I value her. She's a second mother to me, and you are the father I longed to have. To honor both of you, when I have another son, I will give him the name *Shallum*."

Tears of joy flooded Huldah's eyes. "At last we will have a grandson."

"Yes," agreed Josiah as he faced the city wall. "Now let's leave the Hinnom and the sadness of this valley where too many children have burned in the fires of Molech." He preceded them up the path toward the gate.

Supporting each other, Shallum and Huldah followed. Yaphe and a guard of soldiers walked behind them.

A faint glow of dawn tinted the eastern hills. Huldah looked toward the light. "Josiah will continue with his reforms, and the writers of our chronicles will record that he was a good king, that he did what was right in the sight of the Lord as his forefather David did. His descendants will include kings, even a King of kings."

They climbed out of the Hinnom, the valley of death, and entered Jerusalem, the city of life.